Creative Ideas For Lent

ROBERT G. DAVIDSON

CREATIVE IDEAS FOR LENT
Edited by Robert G. Davidson

Copyright © 1985
EDUCATIONAL MINISTRIES, INC.

Scripture quotations unless otherwise noted are from the *Revised Standard Version of the Bible*, copyright © 1946, 1952, and 1971 by the Division of Christian Education of the National Council of Churches.

ISBN 0-940754-25-8
EDUCATIONAL MINISTRIES, INC.

CONTENTS

CHILDREN'S ACTIVITIES 85

INTRODUCTION

This resource has been collected for use as a creative planning aid for Lenten activities in your church. The material has been divided into three major sections: All Church Activities, Children's Activities, and Youth Activities. This does not necessarily mean that the material placed in one section should be limited to that area of programming. For instance, materials might be drawn from all three sections to plan an all church event of projects and learning activities for the whole church family on a Sunday afternoon, followed by an all church dinner and a brief play, then conclude with a short worship service. Or you might want to plan one of these for each of the six Sundays during Lent! Whatever kind of Lenten activity you want to plan, we think you will find something in **CREATIVE IDEAS FOR LENT** to fill your need. So sit down with this book and your staff, do some brain-storming, and plan a meaningful Lenten season for your church. We hope you will be as excited about this Lenten resource as we are!

All Church Activities

CELEBRATION
Symbols of Lent

by Robert G. Davidson

As worship leaders we need to use different methods to awaken our people to the great symbolism which is part of our faith. Richly laden with stories, events, and traditions, the Lenten season provides opportunities to highlight the services of worship by a collage of symbols of the important elements of our Easter faith: (1)palm branches, (2)a bag of money, (3)a basin and towel, (4)grapes and wheat, (5)a crown of thorns, and (6)a handful of nails.

The collage can be as large or as small as you wish, but individual creativity can make a masterpiece of religious art. Different sizes of boxes or flower stands covered with violet colored cloth can make the structure three-dimensional. A seventh symbol, the cross, put in place before the first service, dominates the whole collage. This cross should be constructed from two pieces of rough wood. Each Sunday a symbol is added by three members of the worshiping community (a different trio each week), one reading the suggested sermonette and a second person placing the symbol on the collage, while the third person reads the biblical selection listed and a brief prayer.

Variations of this basic program can be adapted for other settings. Add hymns and expand the sermonettes, and a series of six Sunday evening worship services for Youth Ministry groups emerges. Or prepare the readings so they can be taken home by church school families and used as family vesper services during Lent, each family thus creating their own Holy Week collage just as many families light Advent candles during the Advent season.

FIRST SUNDAY OF LENT

We call the last week of Jesus' earthly life Holy Week. We celebrate the significant events because we never want to forget the possibility of new life which became real at its conclusion. The cruel events of that last week cannot be changed, but we can recall them each year and continue to learn from them.

During the six Sundays of Lent we will be creating a living collage incorporating the symbols of Holy Week. Each week we will add a new symbol to our collage and recall its significance, as we build a pictorial scene during this time of Lent.

Our collage today already has one symbol placed on it — a rough, natural cross which reminds us that as this week ended Jesus suffered and died upon such a cross. A cross which in time became a powerful symbol for Christianity.

On this first Sunday of Lent we place our first symbol—a small palm tree—at the foot of the cross. The branches remind us of Jesus' triumphant entry into Jerusalem on that first Palm Sunday. Of the joy and excitement which was felt as the people saw Jesus coming up the dusty road to their great city, and as he neared they began to sing and wave palm branches. They had great hopes and expectations that this man called Jesus would change their lives.

9

Scripture Reading: Mark 11:8-10

Prayer: Dear God, on this first Sunday of Lent let each of us feel the excitement and joy which people felt as they ran to meet Jesus on that Sunday morning long ago. Amen.

SECOND SUNDAY OF LENT

Lent is a time to remember the life of Jesus and the events of his last week as he taught and healed the people in and about Jerusalem. To help us accomplish this we are creating a living collage of symbols during the weeks of Lent. The cross reminds us of the way the week ended, and the palm branches remind us of how the week began with Jesus' triumphant entry into Jerusalem.

This second Sunday of Lent we add another symbol, a money bag. Early in the week Judas went to the high priest and for 30 pieces of silver agreed to betray Jesus. Judas may have had many reasons for doing this, even perhaps believing the act to be honorable. But the way it turned out, it was not. The money bag reminds us of this tragedy, the betrayal of a trusting friend. But even today we see betrayal taking place in the lives of people around us. We also realize how easy it would be for us to betray a friend. How would we react if we were the betrayed and how would we feel if we became the betrayer?

Let us search our own spirits as we place on the collage the symbol of the money bag.

Scripture Reading: Mark 14:10-11

Prayer: Dear Father, as we see the money bag and come to understand the meaning of a broken relationship, let each of us be aware of the eternal value of trusted friendships. Amen.

THIRD SUNDAY OF LENT

On our collage we now have three symbols—the palm branches and the cross, which represent the events of the beginning and the end of Holy Week, and the money bag, which symbolizes the betrayal of Jesus by his trusted friend, Judas.

On this third Sunday of Lent we add a basin and towel. In washing and drying the feet of his disciples, Jesus took upon himself a servant's task. When Jesus started to perform this task his disciples expressed strong objections for two reasons. Their Master was not supposed to be washing anyone's feet, just as they were not supposed to perform this task. This was the task of servants. How would you feel if you had to wash another person's feet? When Jesus had finished washing his disciples feet, he told them that if they were to follow him, they should not be too proud to serve other persons.

We need to learn humility in serving others and to recall that Jesus came into the world to serve and not to be served. Remembering our call to servanthood, we add a basin and towel to our collage today.

Scripture Reading: John 13:5-8

Prayer: O Lord God, help us to raise our thoughts and actions beyond ourselves to the concern and care of other people—known and unknown to us. Amen.

FOURTH SUNDAY OF LENT

The joy of Palm Sunday was quickly forgotten, and on Thursday evening Jesus gathered with his disciples in the Upper Room.

Today, the fourth Sunday of Lent, we consider other symbols that mark an event in Holy Week—the grapes and wheat. These remind us of the disciples gathered in the Upper Room for the Passover and the Last Supper. The grapes represent the source of the wine which Jesus shared and the wheat stands for the bread he offered. Those persons gathered about that table found new meaning and purpose for their lives. As Jesus took a loaf of bread, the very basis of life, and shared it, he said, "As often as you eat of this bread, do it in remembrance of me."

These symbols still speak to us today as we remember that we are part of his gathered community in this world. The grapes and wheat remind us of the last supper Jesus shared with us and the call to ministry which we accept as members of his community. They also remind us of the deep and abiding love he offered to each of us so freely and which we are called to share with others.

We add to our collage of Holy Week the grapes and the wheat.

Scripture Reading: Matthew 26:26-29

Prayer: Dear God, we are thankful for the community which Jesus, your Son, brought into being. We ask that we have the continuing spirit to be faithful members of that community. Amen.

FIFTH SUNDAY OF LENT

Our Lenten collage bears symbols of events in the life of Jesus during Holy Week: first the palm branches and the triumphant entry he had into the city of Jerusalem, then the money bag and the betrayal by a trusted friend, the basin and towel representing his service and concern for others, and finally the grapes and wheat symbolizing his continuing presence with us.

This fifth Sunday of Lent we think of the Jewish authorities seeking Jesus' crucifixion and the Roman leader, Pilate, submitting to their wishes and to his desire to have this man out of the way. Jesus was led away by the soldiers, who made a crown of thorns and placed it on his head, proclaiming him "King of the Jews." They could not believe this humble man to be the Christ.

By not taking Jesus seriously, we still hurt him today. We find it hard to accept the Good News and to become part of his Kingdom here and now. We find it easier to wait until tomorrow, we have our own things to do today. We want to believe, yet we are still troubled by our unbelief.

We now place a crown of thorns on our living collage.

Scripture Reading: Matthew 27:28-31

Prayer: O Lord God, we would raise our humble prayer this day asking for forgiveness as we find it easier to put off doing that which you have called us to do today. May we move forward in accepting your call to commitment today. Amen.

SIXTH SUNDAY OF LENT

Meaningful symbols make up our Lenten collage. We recall the events at the beginning and the close of Holy Week as we look at the cross and palm branches. We have also placed on our collage a money bag for betrayal, a towel and basin for service, the grapes and wheat for love and community, and the crown of thorns for unbelief.

Today we place on our collage a handful of nails to represent the wrong doings and injustice in our world. Jesus was captured and sentenced to death on the cross. He was forced to carry his wooden cross through the streets of Jerusalem to the place of crucifixion where he was nailed to that same cross.

Through the pain and anguish of that moment—when envy, hate, pride, cruelty all came to a climax—we hear Jesus saying from his cross to every person, "Father, forgive them."

Scripture Reading: John 19:17-18

Prayer: Father, help us to follow Jesus' example of forgiveness in our everyday relationships. How little effort it would take for us to be a little more kind, a little more generous, and a little more patient with those around us. How can we make this world a better place to live? Help us to always keep Jesus' spirit with us in our daily lives and let us never forget the Easter experience. Amen.

FROM THE DIARY OF MARY MAGDALENE

by Elaine Owen Hooley

Too often we read about Passion Week without thinking about Christ and his followers as real people and not just fictional characters. The point of this piece is to help people realize the mixed emotions Christ's death must have caused his friends before they knew of his resurrection.

It has taken me all week to find the time and energy to sit down and record what's happened. It all seems like a bad dream but I know this is one I will never wake up from.

If only things had continued as they were last Sunday when we came to Jerusalem. It finally looked like Jesus had met his goal. Crowds came out to honor him. There were palms and flowers everywhere. For three years Jesus had led a quiet revolution in thought. Love was his message and its fire seemed to finally catch the people. It was all so exciting and yet, even before Sunday, Jesus had been making all kinds of references to the end. I thought Sunday was a new beginning of Jesus' failure and defeat.

On Tuesday Jesus insisted upon going to the temple. We had all heard about the business dealings going on there but Jesus seemed unduly upset. He usually accepted everything in such a peaceful way but this abuse of the house of God infuriated him. I had an awful feeling when he left that morning that this visit to the temple meant trouble. When the disciples told me the things he had done, I could hardly believe it of Jesus. Why he wasn't arrested by the temple guard, I'll never know but this was how the real trouble began.

Wednesday was rather non-eventful, spent mostly in preparing the passover meal. Thursday's get together was a big contrast. The meal went as usual but afterwards Jesus acted so strangely and said such awful things to Peter and Judas. They seemed awful then but somehow he knew they were true. Peter was always such a hot head so I was not surprised when he blew up over Jesus's accusations of betrayal. I don't think Peter ever dreamed that Jesus was right about him. He cried like a baby Friday morning when he told us what he had done. As angry as I was, I also felt sorry for him.

Friday was the worst day I have ever lived. Watching Jesus abused, beaten, humiliated by the same crowd that had praised him was unbelievable. Watching the dearest human being I've ever known slowly and agonizingly die, tore at my very soul. The only thing that hurt more was to watch his mother. Mary is such a beautiful proper lady and to watch her endure the suffering was awful. John tried to get her to leave but she stayed to the end. My poor dear Jesus, right to the end he thought of others, the others who died with him, his mother, and even those who crucified him. It was the loneliness of that cry, "My God, my God, why hast thou forsaken me?" that sent chills down my spine. In all the time I'd known him, he never doubted that God was his father and that He had a plan for him.

Now it is all over. Saturday has come and I have cried until I can cry no more. How could they have killed Jesus, my friend, my teacher, a man I truly loved? He had given me self respect, friendship, dignity, and understanding. He had taught me I had worth and all I could do was stand and watch him suffer alone.

Now all that is left is to go in the morning to put spices on the body. I told Mary I would come with her. It's the least I can do.

All that's left is to wait for tomorrow. I can't believe he is really gone. I can't believe he's dead.

JESUS WEEPS OVER JERUSALEM

by Paul Irwin

"When he came in sight of the city, he wept over it and said, 'If only you had known, on this great day, the way that leads to peace! But no; it is hidden from your sight. For a time will come, when your enemies will set up siege-works against you; they will encircle you and hem you in at every point; they will bring you to the ground, you and your children within your walls, and not leave you one stone standing on another, because you did not recognize God's moment when it came.' " *The New English Bible.* (Luke 19:41-44)

Luke places this dramatic moment just after the "triumphal" entry into Jerusalem, but it is undoubtedly intended to be part of that great event. Let me picture the experience in my own words. The procession moves slowly over the saddle of the Mount of Olives and they at last see the city of Jerusalem, the Holy City, with its past greatness and its present splendor! But for Jesus it now speaks only of tragic failure to understand God's intent. Deeply moved, as he looks upon the magnificent buildings of the Temple, he weeps and in his heart cries out, "If you had known the way of peace, but God's purpose for you is hidden from your sight! Woe is you, City of Zion!"

I am suggesting that Jesus' passion, that is, all the soul-troubling experiences which led up to and included his death on the cross, begins with this event, and that it is appropriate to help our observance of Lent by talking about it, by discussing as Christians about the meaning of weeping—Jesus' weeping and our own.

Of course, to discuss "weeping" with all the following questions to prompt you. would take a whole evening. Therefore, when you have read all the questions feel free to select those which especially speak to you and work with these. Since I prepared this for use as part of an all church lenten dinner program, I wanted everyone to have time to speak especially the children and young people. *Therefore, please avoid any long-winded speeches.* This material might also be used as a special all church study program or copies might be prepared and given for use by families in their homes.

The questions:

1. What does Jesus' weeping over Jerusalem mean to you? Put it into a few words of your own.

2. Do you sometimes weep? Why?

3. How do you feel when you weep? Does it help or make matters worse?

4. What is weeping? Is it shedding tears or is it more than that? (We shed tears when we peel onions.)

5. Recall an occasion of weeping that has had much meaning for you: can you share it tonight at your table?

6. What is happening in your world that causes you to weep (i.e. be concerned)?

7. Are there needs and situations in our immediate and larger world which *ought* to cause us to weep?

13

THE DAY THE SUN DANCED

by Elaine M. Ward

"He is dead! It is over! Our hope is destroyed."

Jesus' friends sat in the dark room, remembering his words and his works, especially his last day, that sad Friday.

"It felt as if the world itself were angry," said one of his friends.

"Yes, I can still hear the thunder growling from the sky and the lightning ripping open the earth. I was afraid," admitted another. "Will it ever be light again?"

The others shook their heads. "No, the sun will never shine again for us. The light of our world is gone."

The men cried, for they missed their friend. They cried because what they had hoped for would now never happen.

The long night was dark with pain, especially the pain of their denial.

"We could have died with him."

"We could have saved him from such a terrible death."

"Why did we disappear and not fight for our friend?"

The dark night of despair was long, but the next day was even longer. The sun did not shine. The world was silent and still.

"It is strange," said one of Jesus' friends in the stillness.

"It is strange indeed," the others agreed.

"We have sinned and done wrong, but *he* taught us God's forgiveness." The men quickly fell on their knees in prayer. That night was the longest yet.

Deep in prayer the men were not aware when Benjamin opened the door into the dark room. Through the open door sunlight flooded the room.

"The sun is dancing," Benjamin cried. "The world is alive again!"

The men opened their eyes, blinking in the bright sunlight. They ran to the window. Some of them rushed outside to see for themselves.

The sun was indeed dancing!

"It is strange," said one of Jesus' friends.

"God is with us," said another.

"The sun is shining. It is a new day. It is a new world! Praise be to God. Christ is risen!" they shouted with joy and hope! And though it is strange, the sun-showered world seemed to reply, "He is risen indeed!"

A SERVICE OF WORSHIP FOR ASH WEDNESDAY

by Wesley Taylor

INTRODUCTION

In some places, especially Europe, portions of the liturgy for a worship service on Ash Wednesday are called THE BURIAL OF THE ALLEUIA. Since Lent is a time of penitence, the alleluia was put aside and the themes of self-examination, confession, serious discipline were stressed. In some services this was dramatically symbolized by placing the alleluia (a banner or other appropriate visual statement) in a coffin, with the affirmation that it would rise again with Christ Jesus at Easter.

Other traditions include a burning of palm branches from the year before, and then placing a mark of ash on the forehead of each worshipper. You may want to do this later on in the service during the silent prayer or the singing of the hymn, O MASTER, LET ME WALK WITH THEE. This may be called the LITANY OF ASHES.

A SERVICE OF WORSHIP FOR

ASH WEDNESDAY FOR ALL AGES

CONSIDER

In the Christian tradition the season of Lent — the six weeks preceding Easter plus the last four days of another week beginning today, Ash Wednesday — is a time to make a special spiritual pilgrimage. It is a time of introspection and self-examination when we probe deeply and respond honestly to how we are getting on with the process of transformation into a new person in Jesus Christ.

CALL TO WORSHIP

Leader: Jesus says, The Spirit of the Lord is upon me, because he has chosen me,
Community: to bring good news to the poor. He has sent me to proclaim liberty to the captives, and
Leader: recovery of sight to the blind. To announce the time for the Lord to save his people has come.
Community: We have come, to worship and pray, to praise and remember, and to accept our ministry of discipleship.

SINGING   "When I Survey the Wondrous Cross"

A LITANY OF DISCIPLESHIP

> **Leader:** Lord, I've stayed too long
> on the flat plains of spiritual monotony
> and plunged too often into the valleys of gloom.
> **Community:** Now, for these forty days,
> let me scale the mountain top
> where I can breathe the fresh air
> and see clearly the distant landscape.
> **All:** Let me climb the mountain and meet you there. Amen.

SILENT PRAYER AND CONFESSION

CHILDREN'S STORY

> Father Damien using the story of his life
> DAMIEN AND THE ISLAND OF SICKNESS
> (Kenneth Christopher, Winston Press, 1979)
>
> (Or another story of your choice)

PRAYER OF CONFESSION

As we mark the season of remembrance of the life and passion of our Lord, we pray to you, Father forgive us our folly and excess, our coldness to human sorrow, our envy of those who prosper and are at ease, our passion for things of the moment that perish in the grasping, our indifference to those treasures of the Spirit which are life and peace, our neglect of wise and gracious laws. Heal us, but with the painful understanding of how our hands nail the Son of God to the cross again, exposing him to public shame; through Jesus Christ our Lord. Amen.

WORDS OF ASSURANCE

THE PRELUDE TO THE BURIAL

Reader #1: Alleluia! The Lord's name be praised!
Let the people shout the word.

Reader #2: Alleluia is our song; for the Lord has
worked wondrously to save his people.

HYMN   "All Creatures of Our God and King" (verses 1-3 in hymnal)

verse 4: O friends, in gladness, let us sing, Eternal anthems echoing, Alleluia, Alleluia. To God the Father, God the Son, And God the Spirit, Three in One, Alleluia, Alleluia! Alleluia! Alleluia! Alleluia!

16

Reader #3: Our hearts are filled with joy, but soon that joy
will be taken from us. Jesus told his disciples:
"Where I am going you cannot follow me now; but you
shall follow me afterward." (John 13:36b, RSV)

Reader #1: Peter said to him, "Lord, why cannot I follow you
now? I will lay down my life for you."

Reader #3: Jesus answered, "Will you lay down your life for me?
Truly, truly I say to you, the cock will not crow till
you have denied me three times. (But) let not your hearts
be troubled; believe in God, believe also in me."

Reader #2: Because of Jesus' life, death, and Resurrection, our
lives become fully transformed.

Reader #1: He is with us wherever we may go. Even when we feel
the most distant from him, he is with us; even in
the Valley of the Shadow of Death.

Reader #3: He is with us. We are with him. So we remember his
suffering and death. Take the Alleluia from us.

Reader #2: Take down all the colors of rejoicing and replace them
with the purple of penitential preparation.

(You may want to have a banner up with a joyful theme,
at this point take the banner down to symbolize the change from joy to penitence)

Reader #3: For if we are to rise with Christ, we must die to our
own selves.

THE BURIAL OF THE ALLELUIA

Reader #1: The Alleluia is taken from us, and we wear the dressings
of sorrow.

SILENT PRAYER (may include litany of ashes)

HYMN   "O Master, Let Me Walk With Thee"

Reader #2: No more will there be Alleluias on our lips until that
morn when our Christ is raised Son of God in power.

Reader #3: Then how shall we wait?

Reader #1: Watch and pray.

Reader #2: Watch and pray that you will not enter into
temptation.

Reader #3: Watch and pray that you will be faithful
disciples.

People: Lord, you know what is best for me.
Give me what you will
and when you will
and as much as you will.
Do with me as you know best, Lord,
and as it pleases you
and brings you the most honor.
Place me where you will
and guide me according to your wisdom.
I am in your hand
as your servant
ready to do all that you command.
I want to live
not for myself,
but for you alone.
I want to live worthily
and profitably   -Thomas a'Kempis
and to your honor.

MARK 8: 27-35

(The congregation will then pray in silence.)   O Christ, the Master Carpenter, who at the very end,   through wood and nails,   purchased our whole salvation, wield well your tools in the workshop of your world, so that we, who come rough-hewn to your bench, may here be fashioned to a truer beauty of your hand. We ask it for your own name's sake. Amen.

SINGING "Jesu, Jesu"

GOING FORTH

Leader: Jesus said, "Take up my cross, and follow me."
Community: Yet his yoke is easy, and the burden light,
for his spirit is with us.
Leader: The blessings of God the Creator, the Redeemer, and
the Comforter go with us all.
Community: Amen.

FOR YOUR INFORMATION

The liturgical color for Lent is purple. In ancient times, purple was reserved for royalty. Not only was it too expensive a dye for the common people, it was actually forbidden by law in Rome to any but those who were in the aristocracy. The color, though, for the church has come to express penitence as a sign of preparation. It's as though in preparing to meet the King, we realize how unworthy we are.

18

SEASONS OF THE CHURCH YEAR

BY Jannel Glennie

ADVENT — waiting - preparing - when will He come? - expecting college board results? - a raise? - acceptance? - patience - purple.

CHRISTMAS— birth - beginning - He has come! - relief - joy - new job - a new love - discovery of direction - celebrate - white.

EPIPHANY — manifestation - let it be known - Indeed, He has arrived! - birth announcements - honeymoon - entry - changed life - some joy, some concern - green.

LENT — what now? - reality - He will not be with us long - preparation - purple - will she love me when she discovers my faults? - not quite like I expected - rejection - they don't understand me! - loneliness - depression - nothingness - black.

EASTER — a new day - new life - He lives! - can I truly believe it? - she loves me! - they accepted my proposal - pure joy - white.

PENTECOST — integration - reality accepted - He lives on with renewed Spirit - the long haul - healing - acceptance - deepened relationships - green.

As we move through the seasons of the church year, the seasons move through us. As we plot our faith journey or review our life, the sequence of the seasons appears. If we look long enough, we can also see that, like the church year, that moves in cycles, so too, do our lives. No longer do we need to fear being back where we were two years ago. We can take comfort from the realization that as we move in circles, each year building on the next, like a spiral, we can never be where we were before. There is too much experience in-between to allow that to happen.

We can also take comfort from the fact that when we experience a sacrificial Lenten time in our lives, heading toward the inevitable crucifixion, we know there will be a Easter. Somehow, we can bear the cross - looking for the rock rolled away. But too often we linger on the cross wanting to jump immediately down to greet the women. What about the time in the tomb? We say "He descended to the death." The time in the tomb is a deathly, lonely place. Yet, still we linger not wanting to accept the reality of the crucifixion event — a rejection. If we can believe that Easter is near, perhaps we can release the cross and the tomb, and, miraculously, the stone rolls away.

This is not the end, however, Pentecost is near, and Jesus comes back to spend time with his friends — a reassuring time. He even shows Thomas that, yes, he was wounded, but there is healing that follows. He leaves them for the last time, and in his place the power of the Spirit is made known. No doubt, it had always been there, but at this time its presence is clear and immediate. The work begins. There is time for healing in the season of Pentecost; time to reflect and integrate experiences; and, time to do those things we are called to do.

After a time, we sense new yearnings. Something is about to happen, but we may not be able to name it. It is a time of expectancy — an Advent. Then, the new baby — the new job — beginning of college —arrives. We celebrate Christmas. We share the news and enjoy the rush of emotions that follows. It is the Epiphany.

There is one caution, however, with the analogy of the church seasons and our lives. It is the trap we can fall into with any organized description to how life or faith progresses. We may be tempted to quickly move ourselves on to a "better" stage; or, we might halt or impede the process by refusing to accept reality or hesitating to take a risk. The season we are currently in is the right one for us; and, we need to allow ourselves to be there. It is by God's grace and our faith that we move along through the seasons of our lives.

What can we gain by mixing the met-

aphors of our lives with the events of Christ's life and the history of the church? We can gain understanding and appreciation of all phases of our lives. We may be able to allow ourselves to move deeply into the feelings of rejection/crucifixion, instead of resisting and prolonging the time. We can take time to truly celebrate the Christmases and Easters of our lives. We can be thankful for the long healing and integration time of Pentecost. We can use the preparation times of Advent and Lent to the fullest, aware of the joy in the season to follow.

Understanding our lives in reference to the church seasons gives us many new possibilities: reassurance, confidence, hope, strength , perserverance. Most of all, however, it gives us a connectedness with our God. It gives us a way to know God better through His Son and through His Spirit.

Discussion questions:

Take a moment to reflect on your life or faith journey. You may wish to plot it on a life line or draw the hills and valleys of experiences.

Choose one experience. Which of the church seasons or events in the church year connects with this experience? What events led up to the event? followed the event? Again, relate them to the church year. Notice any similarities or differences. What scriptural event is similiar to your experience?

In what season do you find yourself now? What scriptural event is similiar to your current experiences?

Begin to picture this scriptural story. Using all your senses, place yourself in the story. Who are the characters? Where is it happening? What is happening? What interaction do you have with the story? How does the story end?

How may your view have changed about the current situation or experience? What can you do to better appreciate the season in which you find yourself?

LENTEN FASTIVITY

by Mark Watkins

Passing quickly through the halls of a local hospital, I came to a screeching halt upon seeing a sign posted on a patient's door. In bold cursive it read, "Fasting For The Hospital". The words echoed in my mind. Flashing across my thoughts came this response, "Sure, these days we'll fast for hospital tests, yet forget how people of faith once fasted for the Lord, our Creator, Sustainer!"

This rather shocking revelation parted my 'dead sea', some of those long lost, unused brain cells. Less engrossed with my purpose for being on this particular hospital floor, I moved on to make a pastoral visit with a 'pre-op' patient. But I was unable to concentrate on my task of comforting the person; the words "Fasting For The Hospital" continued to usurp all of my energies and attention.

Bill Cosby, in one of his comic bits, mentioned the time he had a car accident. In short, Bill described what happened to the police officer in the following manner, "Well, you see, a tree jumped out and grabbed my tires and made me crash."

I know what Bill Cosby is talking about. A simple sign entered my life one day, messing up my effectiveness and grabbing my whole being to the very core. A feeling of loss or emptiness surged. Thus this group worship experience, Lenten Fastivity, was created.

The anointed one, Jesus the Christ, fasted for forty days in the wilderness following his exciting baptism by John. Jesus abstained from eating food and most assuredly used this time to subdue his body to his spiritual purpose on earth.

Fasting exists as an outward sign of penitence repenting one's wrong doings. It also happens to be used as a personal spiritual challenge in seeking out the answer to one's mission in this world and how one best taps into the Holy Spirit.

Here are some suggestions for the following worship service. On the first day of Lent, Ash Wednesday, encourage your group to hold a brief worship service enabling them to experience fasting in a new light. Approximately one hour in length, its emphasis is accentuated if the service occurs in the sanctuary or chapel. You will need: three white candles, large metal bowl, song books or sheets, paper, pencils, and matches. Worship leaders need Bibles.

AN ORDER OF WORSHIP

Producing the Ashes

Begin in a chosen meeting room, writing down on small sheets of paper, things which you are sorry for doing. Add to that something you wish to achieve in your lifetime which you think will help present the God we worship best to other people. Everyone fold these sheets, putting them into the metal bowl. Have the Worship Leader say a prayer over the many contributions. Take the bowl outside and light the papers. Let it burn until all that remains are ashes.

Procession

Everyone walks slowly to the sanctuary singing "We Are One In The Spirit". Carry the bowl of ashes placing it upon the table with three candles.

21

Memory Lights

A Worship Leader, when everyone has taken a seat, lights three white candles saying, "We light these candles which symbolize God, Job, and Jesus. Both Job and Jesus fasted at some point in their lives. We too will have the opportunity to experience this powerful abstinence on Saturday. May the Lord watch over us as we seek to listen to His will when we fast and while we worship."

Scripture Readings
    Job 42:1-6
    Matthew 6:16-18

A Brief History of Old and New Testament Fasting

Old Testament- Without mentioning origin, fasts recorded in the Bible were periods of no food or drink. What a sacrifice? We are not talking about just certain kinds of food, but all kinds of food available to those peoples. For us this means no pizza, carbonated drinks, steaks, cheeseburgers and french fries, etc. Nothing! How did they do it? Maybe we will learn.

Well, "First, there were certain annual fasts Thus Hebrews fasted on the Day of Atonement (Leviticus 16:29-31; 23:27-32; Numbers 29:7). After the Exile, four other annual fasts were observed all of them according to the Talmud, marked disaster in Jewish history..."[1]

The Hebrews used fasting as a form of expressing grief and seeking the forgiveness of God. Those who sought God's guidance and strength also fasted, whether individually or in a corporate body of faith.

New Testament- Surprisingly enough, the Day of Atonement, an annual fast of the Hebrews, gets the greatest attention in the New Testament (Acts 27:9). Monday and Thursday were strict fasting days for a certain school of Pharisees. Anna gained mention for fasting quite often in Luke 2:37.

What about Jesus' view of fasting? Didn't the devil tempt him in the wilderness, a preparatory period before Jesus started his ministry? Maybe he keyed off of Moses and Elijah, men of God?

Jesus assumed that his hearers would fast, but taught them when they did so to face Godward, not manward (Matthew 6:16-18). When asked why his disciples did not fast as did those of John the Baptist and of the Pharisees, Jesus did not repudiate fasting, but declared it to be innappropriate for his disciples 'as long as the bridegroom is with them' (Matthew 9:14-17; Mark 2:18-22; Luke 5:33-39). Later, they would fast, like others. [2]

Parting Remarks and Prayer

The fast which takes place on Saturday is personal. You are asked not to eat food. You may drink as much water as desired. If any physical problem hinders you from fasting, then do not participate. Please come to church Sunday to share what your experience was like with other members of the congregation. We will have a discussion about your experience and observations of fasting.

Let us pray: Lord, grant that we might learn more about You each and every day. Be with us especially as we fast for You this weekend. Amen.

[1] *The New Bible Dictionary* by J.D. Douglas, Or. Ed., William B. Eerdmans Pub. Co., Grand Rapids, MI, 1977, page 418.

[2] Ibid., page 419.

PASS ON THE PASSOVER

by Colleen Britton

Before we can fully appreciate all that Holy Week means we need to understand the hopes, the faith, and the expectations that were all a part of the Passover celebration at the time of Christ. As our understanding of Passover grows, so does our understanding and appreciation of all that Christ did and said during that last week. His words and actions take on even deeper meaning when we understand the traditions and the meanings of the symbols he used.

The first Passover in Egypt, about the year 1250 B.C., marked the end of 400 years of slavery for Israel. Through this first Passover experience, the lives of the Hebrew first born were saved by the blood of a lamb, and the people were led with hope into a new land of promise. These events demonstrated God's power, his saving grace, and his continuing faithfulness to Israel.

Since the time of the Exodus, the annual Passover celebration has been the most important Jewish holiday, and it perpetuates the importance and the impact of the Passover events on the lives of successive generations. The Passover continues to be a celebration of sacrifice, deliverance, thanksgiving, remembrance, and a promise of future deliverance.

The Passover is both an actual meal and a sacramental meal. The foods eaten are symbols of spiritual truths and past events. Over the years it evolved into a long and more formal ceremony with special prayers, the reciting of several psalms, and ceremonial handwashings. But the focus of the meal always has been on the "Haggadah", the retelling of the Exodus story. The story unfolds as the host answers four questions which are asked by the youngest son.

Your congregation, church school class, or youth group can participate in an informal dialogue centered around the Passover table, and learn to appreciate the meaning and symbolism that surround this ancient celebration. The Passover meal itself is an "intergenerational" learning experience. Even in the earliest days, the Passover meal was planned as a family gathering, a time when young and old would gather around the table and hand down faith and tradition from one generation to the next.

For your Passover table you will need a goblet of wine, a small bowl of salt water, and a Sedar plate, a large plate which is placed at the center of the table. The Sedar plate contains a sample of the traditional Passover foods; matzos, or unleaven bread, lamb bones, bitter herbs, parsley, horseradish, charoseth, a mixture of finely chopped apples, nuts, dates, cinnamon, and wine, and a roasted egg. Prepare extra food to pass around for tasting. This can be placed on one or more trays, or small individual containers, whatever seems convenient for your group.

Invite the children to sit around the table and lean on it with one elbow throughout the meal. Explain that the meaning of the Passover story will unfold as they ask the four traditional questions and the father, or host, aided by the rest of the group, answers them.

QUESTION ONE: On all other nights we can eat any kind of bread. On this night, why only unleavened bread?

First of all, do the children know what leaven is? You may want to have some packets of leaven and a loaf of leavened bread for them to examine. Compare it to matzo which is like a flat cracker. How long does it take for bread dough with yeast in it to rise? Bread dough without leaven can be baked as soon as it is mixed.

The reason that only unleavened bread is eaten at the Passover is because on this night we remember that the Hebrews had to be ready to leave Egypt quickly. There was no time to wait for the bread to rise.

For seven days before the Passover, Jews don't eat leavened bread, and they remove all forms of leaven from their house. A favorite part of the Passover is the search for leaven, where the children search through the house for any possible leaven. Usually the mother will have hidden a small piece of matzo which becomes a prize.

There is another reason that Jews removed leaven from their homes during Passover. Natural leaven is a form of bacteria which causes fermentation, and in Old Testament times it symbolized corruption, uncleanness, and evil.

Have the children remove any leaven or leavened bread from the room.

The leavened bread or matzo is called the bread of affliction or suffering. When it is broken during the first part of the meal, everyone eats only a tiny piece as a reminder that as slaves the Hebrews ate only crumbs.

Break off a piece of matzo and pass it around, asking everyone to eat only a tiny crumb.

QUESTION TWO: On all other nights we eat herbs or vegetables of any kind. On this night why do we eat only bitter herbs?

On this night we eat the bitter herbs to recall that the Egyptians embittered the lives of our forefathers in Egypt with hard labor. They were forced to make mortar and bricks, and did every other kind of work in the fields. It was a hard, bitter time.

The bitter herbs can include parsley, horseradish, chicory, endive, or lettuce. The parsley has several meanings. It is symbolic of spring and renewal, and it is also a reminder of hyssop, the brush-like plant that was used to paint the door posts with the blood of a lamb.

QUESTION THREE: On all other nights we do not dip our herbs or vegetables even once; on this night, why do we dip them twice?

We dip the herbs in salt water to recall the tears that our forefathers shed in Egypt. The salt water is also a reminder of the water of the Sea of Reeds that the Hebrews crossed when they left Egypt.

We dip the herbs in charoseth to recall how the lives of our forefathers were embittered by their hard labor. The charoseth is a mixture of apples, nuts, dates, cinnamon and wine, and represents the mortar and the bricks without straw that the Israelite slaves made in Egypt. The charoseth has a very sweet taste, and reminds us that life is often a bitter/sweet experience. No matter how bitter the dark appears, we should look forward to better days. The charoseth or "sop" as it was sometimes called, symbolizes hope.

Do you remember that when Jesus was at the table with his disciples during the Last Supper, he dipped a morsel into the "sop" and gave it to Judas? The "sop" was the charoseth. Let children dip the herbs in salt water and charoseth.

QUESTION FOUR: On all other nights we eat our meals in any manner; on this night why do we sit around the table in a reclining position?

24

In Biblical times people generally ate standing, sitting or squating on the floor. Only princes or rulers sat on couches. But for the Passover meal, the Hebrews ate in a reclining position, resting on low cushions or pillows, and eating from a low table as a reminder of the rest which God gave to them after He redeemed them from bondage. Often, even today, they will use a small pillow and lean on the table as they eat the Passover.

Pick up the remaining foods on the Sedar plate and explain their meaning.

The lamb bone, usually a lamb shank, is a reminder of the lamb which was sacrificied at the first Passover when its blood was painted on the door posts to protect the Hebrews from the angel of death. In Jesus' time, the unblemished lamb was sacrificied at the Temple, and then taken home and eaten. The roasted lamb was the main course of the meal, and it all had to be eaten that night — no leftovers.

The egg has always been a symbol of life and at the Passover meal it represents the life of the firstborn who was saved by God. It reminds the Hebrews that all their first born males are dedicated to God and belong to Him.

The ten plagues are remembered during the Passover meal as we dip one finger in the wine, and place one drop of wine on the plate for every plague. Name the plagues out loud as you put each drop on the plate, and see how many your group can remember. (water turned to blood, frogs, gnats, flies, death of cattle, boils, hail locusts, darkness, death of Egyptian first born.)

Four glasses of wine are drunk during the Passover meal, and prayers are said before each one. Each cup of wine represents one of the promises God made to Moses in Exodus 6:6-7. "I will deliver you from the burdens of the Egyptians. I will redeem you with outstretched arms and with great acts. I will take you for my people, and I will be your God. I will bring you to the land which I swore to give to Abraham, Isaac and Jacob, and I will give it

to you for a possession." The first cup of wine is called the cup of sanctification and separates the meal from all common meals. The second cup is called the cup of the "haggadah" or "telling". After this cup was drunk, the head of the house tells the whole story of the Passover and ends with an admonition that in every generation one must look upon himself as if he personally had come out from Egypt. For it was not only our forefathers whom the Holy One redeemed. He redeemed us too... Therefore, it is our duty to thank and to praise Him in song and prayer; to glorify and extol Him who performed all these wonders for our forefathers and for us.

After the main course of the meal has been eaten, prayers are said again over the bread and the rest of it is eaten. Then after prayers of thanksgiving, the final cup of wine is drunk and psalms of praise are sung. Usually these include Psalms 113-118 which are known as the "Hallel", meaning "the praise of God". Psalm 118 is known as the Great Hallel and is ususally sung at the closing of the Passover meal.

It was during this final part of the Passover meal that Jesus took the bread and the cup of wine and gave them new meaning and symbolism. Jesus identified himself with the Passover symbols which were already reminders of sacrifice and deliverance. He proclaimed that through his sacrifice, men would find deliverance from the bondage of sin.

Have children serve Passover trays to the rest of the group. Suggest that they make a sandwich with matzos, herbs, charoseth, and chopped egg. Encourage them to think about the symbols and the meanings behind each food. If they can't remember, encourage them to ask the person next to them.

While the group is being served, ask for any other questions or thoughts about the Passover that some might like to share.

When all have been served, close with a prayer and the singing of a hymn such as "Guide Me O Thou Great Jehovah".

STORY SHARING

by Judith Frenz

This can be scheduled as a part of a midweek Lenten worship or as an additional Lenten night event.

Before the congregational group gathers, prepare a room for story-telling. Construct a story-telling circle by arranging chairs in a circle around a low table. (If the floor is carpeted provide the opportunity for those who wish to sit on the floor.) Make the circle large enough to accomodate 10-12 participants but close enough to produce a feeling of intimacy. Make as many story circles as needed. On the low table place a number of votive and other candles in assorted holders. (If necessary, this can be done in the same room as the rest of the evening's activities. However, it would be preferable to use a separate room.)

Also prepare a room large enough for a congregational potluck meal. At the end of this room arrange two of the long tables with supplies for an art project. Place a long strip of newsprint or a large paper tablecloth on one table. At the top, print or cut out letters to form the phrase "Jesus, Our Savior." On the other table put scissors , construction paper, old worship bulletins, partially used lesson books, glue, markers, glitter, or any art supplies you think someone might wish to use.

Begin the evening with a fellowship potluck meal. After everyone has eaten, the co-ordinator takes the group to the story-telling room or area. (Have the candles lit and all other room lights turned off.)

As soon as everyone is seated comfortably in the story circles, let the story-telling begin. The co-ordinator guides the story-telling so that the group tells "my story", "your story", and "God's story". First have the oldest member of the story circle tell a favorite Bible story. Then ask the youngest storyteller who can talk to tell one. After allowing others in the circle to share stories as they wish, move on to asking each member to relate how someone—a past storyteller—has influenced their Christian faith and life. Concluding with sharing "A time when you influenced someone else by being a storyteller."

When the story-telling period has ended, have the entire group return to where the art supplies are located. There they can relate and reinforce learnings by making a group mural. Direct the participants to contribute words and pictures that they feel relate to and illustrate the theme of Jesus, Our Savior.

Fasten the completed mural to the wall for congregational viewing. Then close the session with a prayer or short period of worship.

Be sure and provide an area where little ones can take a break from the events. However, make every effort to involve them in the activities. Many great truths come from the mouths and hands of babes.

"HAVE JOY,

WILL TRAVEL"

by Rudy H. Thomas

One tradition has it that the very tomb in which Jesus was buried is now deep in the confines of the Church of the Holy Sepulchre in the heart of Jerusalem. At dawn each Easter morning a specially selected youth from ancient Palestine reaches a candle into an opening in the tomb and when he withdraws it everyone is overjoyed to see that the candle has been lighted. As the young man turns to light the candles held by other youth he shouts, "Hallelujah, Christ is risen!" These young people hurry on to light candles held by still other youth in the streets and villages always shouting, "Hallelujah, Christ is risen!"

Several years ago a professional guide was telling a group of tourists about this impressive yearly event. One of the tourists said to the guide: "But surely, *this year*, with all the troubles here in the mideast, this traditional candlelighting will be postponed."

"No, no," said the guide, "this year by all means, more than ever!"

Well, this year, with the mideast once again a tinder box which could explode any day, "this year, more than ever." Easter needs to be celebrated in the Holy Land and in our land.

The Scottish preacher, David Cairns, once said, "The resurrection is the land where the great mists lie, but it is also the land where the great rivers spring." There is much about the resurrection we do not understand, but here is also unbelievable joy and hope that springs forth in a believer on Easter.

Dr. Paul Tillich told us that the word "resurrection" is not a good translation from the Aramaic. He said we really ought to talk about the "new being." The new being is that

out of something which is distorted and bent, stained and bruised, God can fashion something new and wonderful. This is one of the most powerful themes of the Bible. The idea of the resurrection is that no matter what the circumstances God can take the old and make a new you.

We need to think more about the quality of our life now than of what life may be like after death. In a way the New Testament is saying that "tomorrow is today and today is forever." It says that you experience eternal life now, not after you die. Jesus said, "Whosoever lives and believes in me shall never die." I believe that means whoever grasps something of the quality of his life ... whoever reflects his love this moment, this day moves from life that is death to life that is eternal.

There is a wonderful story of a little girl who changed a whole town's attitude of gloom, including the attitude of her own pastor who was given to preaching much hell fire and damnation. One day Pollyanna told him he ought to get more joy into his preaching since the Bible itself was full of joy. The minister stayed up all night and by actual count discovered the Bible has some 826 passages concerning joy.

If you want to know joy that has the quality of eternity in it then get the love of Christ working in and through your life. Get

27

out of yourself, stop resisting taking any responsibility in the life of your church, stop hating other people, throw yourself into some good works in the church and the community. In short, be a lover of people and ask God to help you meet the needs of people. And don't think for one moment that eternal joy in your life is dependent on good health, or easy and trouble-free times. It|is troubled and broken hearts and sickness that often awakens in persons a deep feeling of eternal joy.

A colleague and friend of mine received a letter from a dear friend and colleague of his. After some opening remarks he wrote:

"I am seriously ill with cancer and do not know how long I will live. Perhaps five to ten years if I am lucky. Perhaps longer. Perhaps not so long. But my faith is strong that God's love is around me and my wife and three children.

"It is in this vein that I wrote, for I read a statement some weeks ago by a young man in your church asking 'Why?' about the joyous things, the *good things*. James Christensen wrote that 'we have no right to ask "Why?" of all life's *bad experiences* unless we also ask "Why?" of all life's *joyous and good ones.*'

"I agree. I hope that young man will also. I am working mostly full time. Please understand that my illness has also been a *blessing* for me and my family - we are closer - and for the congregation, we are more honest and we seem to choose priorities better.

"Pray for me as I will pray for you! Your friend in Christ."

Eternal joy in *our lifetime* does not depend on good health or easy, troublefree times. What every man and woman needs to understand is that life *in the body* and death|*of the body* are both gifts of God.

Several years ago a woman died in Wooster. She had suffered long from the ravages of cancer. Yet she died full of the celebration of life. As she prepared to face her own death she wrote a series of poems. Let me share some of her poems with you.

The kiss of death
Has wakened me
To LIFE,
I did not see,
Nor hear,
Nor feel,
As I do now.

Death's touch,
Life a lover's caress,
Has left me
Shaken
With the beauty
Of LIFE.

And this beautiful testimony of how a present quality of life can lead to an eternal joy:

I will travel
Light
As I journey
Toward the sunrise.

Who needs envy,
Self-pity,
Fear?

They're too heavy for me.
Without them
I feel buoyant,
Light.

HAVE JOY
WILL TRAVEL.

THAT'S WHAT EASTER IS ALL ABOUT, AN ETERNAL JOY....
HALLELUJAH!

GOOD FRIDAY HAPPENING

by Jane Priewe

A responsive reading which can be used between male and female, children and adults, or leader and congregation.

Psalm 54:

Reader 1: After Pontius Pilate had handed Jesus over to be crucified, he was taken by soldiers to a hill outside the city. Romans called the hill Calvary. The Jews called the hill Golgotha. Today the place of Christ's crucifixion is still called 'Skull Hill'', because it bears a resemblance to a human skull.

Reader 2: I am the cross Christ took on his back. That long ago day when skies grew black. Weary from a night of agony he fell on the way to Calvary. To carry me for the Nazarene Soldiers singled out Simon of Cyrene.

Hymn: "When I Survey The Wondrous Cross"

(Sung by a group or by everyone.)

Reader 3: Jesus was nailed to the cross on Calvary, and two thieves were crucified with him; the one on his right hand, and the other on his left. The scripture was fulfilled,"And he was numbered with the transgressors." During this time until Jesus died, he was mocked and taunted by priests, scribes, and elders, as well as by people who came to watch. While Christ suffered on the cross, soldiers gambled for his clothes.

Reader 4:
(Three or four voice choir needed for this recitation.)

We are Christ's garments tossed on the ground at the base of his cross in a pile. While they cast lots for us, soldiers made not a sound, when they won, they would whistle and smile.

Isaiah 53:12
(Read by all.)

Reader 5: During the last few hours of Jesus' life such strange and frightening things happened, it was as though God presented a pageant of His almighty power. Stunned by things he felt and saw but could not explain, the officer of the Roman soldiers said, 'Truly this man was the Son of God.'

Reader 6: I am the darkness that fell over the earth. I'm not sure what was God's plan. Perhaps it was His way of turning His face. To hide the evil of man!

Reader 7: I am the earth that rumbled and shook. I made buildings rattle and groan. I bucked and rolled like a ship in a storm. People knew it was time to atone.

Reader 8: Inside the temple, I am the veil which ripped from ceiling to floor. Although my cloth was as thick as your hand, like tissue paper, I tore!

Luke 23:47-49
(Read by all.)

Reader 9: Jesus utters his last words on the cross and dies. While on the cross he has spoken words of mercy and of kindness. He has asked for God's help during his suffering. Now, relief and joy ring in his words as he dies.

Reader 10:
(Three or four voice choir needed for this recitation.)

"Father, into Thy hands I commend my spirit." We are those last words Christ said. And hearing, folks knew he was the Son of God. Each trembled and bowed his head.

Hymn: "Throned Upon the Awful Tree"

Reader 11: Once he had died, Jesus' friends moved quickly to claim his body, so he could be buried before nightfall. Joseph of Arimathea and Nicodemus, both members of the Sanhedrin, received permission from Pontius Pilate to bury their Savior. Christ was laid to rest in a tomb hewn out of rock in which Joseph of Arimathea had planned to be buried. As soon as the body was inside, a heavy stone was rolled in place to block the tomb's opening.

Reader 12: I am the tomb where Christ was laid, in a garden not far from Calvary. A winding sheet of pure white cloth was wrapped 'round the man from Galilee. Then leaving the tomb, Joseph blocked the door to seal the silent, dark cavity. The Sabbath arrived, as darkness dropped o'er Jerusalem in silent gravity.

Mark 15:43-46
(Read by all.)

Hymn: "We Sing The Praise of Him Who died"

30

THE LENTEN CROSS

by Colleen Britton

Just as the Advent Wreath with its four candles helps us remember the significance of Advent, the Lenten Cross with its six candles helps us remember and understand the meaning of Lent. Originally, the Lenten Cross was made from the wood of the Christmas tree. Thus it served as a reminder that the same Jesus whose birth we celebrate at Christmas was later crucified on the cross as a man. Six purple candles represent the six weeks of Lent and a white Christ candle in the center symbolizes Easter. Purple is a color which denotes royalty. It also symbolizes repentance and a time of preparation. The white Christ candle symbolizes purity, and joy.

Before each candle is lit, a brief meditation or lesson adds to our understanding of what Lent means. The Lenten Cross can become a learning tradition for your congregation both during worship services and around the family table. Below are meditation suggestions for each of the six weeks. These can be used with children during worship services, church school, children's church, or youth group worship services. There are hundreds of other possibilities to make each week of Lent a meaningful time of Christian growth.

FIRST SUNDAY: *LENT: A TRADITIONAL TIME OF PREPARATION FOR EASTER*

What is Lent? The word "Lent" comes form the Latin word meaning "springtime" or the "lengthening of days". It's a period of 40 days (excluding Sundays) prior to Easter. (40 days because Moses, Jesus and other Biblical characters went into the wilderness for 40 days to prepare for various tasks.)

Lent is a Christian tradition, a time to PREPARE, to get ready for Easter. What is a tradition? It is the handing down of information, beliefs, and customs by word of mouth or by example from one generation to another without written instruction. A TRADITION IS A WAY OF LEARNING BY DOING.

So Lent is a way of learning, a way of becoming a better Christian by doing and practicing certain things. Each week of Lent we are going to talk briefly about something Lent means and something you can DO to help you grow as a Christian:

This week everyone will receive a list of 40 THINGS TO DO DURING LENT. Each activity will help you prepare for Easter and will help you grow as a Christian. Pass out Lenten calendar's with 40 activities for them to do, one each day of Lent. *(See page 34)*

Light the first candle on the Lenten Cross (bottom one) as we remember that LENT IS A TIME OF PREPARATION AND GROWTH, AS WE LEARN BY DOING.

SECOND SUNDAY: *DO GOOD DEEDS/SHOW KINDNESS*

What is a good deed? Think of some examples. Jesus teaches us to love one another and to be kind to one another. He and his disciples spent their lives serving others, caring for the sick and comforting the lonely and those in sorrow. The Bible tells us to "Be doers of the word, and not hearers only" (James 1:22). This means that since we know Jesus' teachings about loving and caring for one another, we ought to PRACTICE CARING, HELPING, SHARING -- doing good deeds and showing kindness, just as Jesus did. Pass out cross lapel pins to be worn upside down until they do a good deed, then they turn them right side up.

Light the second candle: DO GOOD DEEDS/ SHOW KINDNESS.

THIRD SUNDAY: *GIVING/ SACRIFICE*

How many like presents? Do you ever give presents to people? Whenever we give a present to someone, it costs us something -- either money if we buy it, or time and energy if we make it. Whenever someone does something nice for you, buys you a present, cooks you dinner, takes you out to eat, remember that the gift is a sacrifice -- it cost the person something, either money, time, or energy, or all three.

God gave us his Son, Jesus, as a gift to show us the greatness of his love. That gift of love cost Jesus his life, a sacrifice he willingly made. We can learn what sacrifice means by giving up something we have or want in order to make someone else happy.

This morning we're going to give each one of you a dollar. The only catch is, that you use it to MAKE SOMEONE ELSE HAPPY. Next week you can share with us some of the things you did.

Light the third candle of GIVING AND SACRIFICE.

FOURTH SUNDAY: *FORGIVENESS*

Have you ever done anything that you knew you shouldn't? We all have at one time or another. How did you feel? Was it hard for you to tell your parents or friend that you were sorry? How did they respond? Then how did you both feel? (BETTER! Things were back to normal.)

In the Lord's Prayer Jesus taught us that God will forgive us for the things we do that are wrong in the same way that we forgive others for the things that they do wrong to us.

This week remember to forgive others, and ask God to forgive you for the wrongs you do. Don't be afraid to say, "I am sorry."

Let's say the Lord's Prayer together and then we'll light the fourth candle: FORGIVENESS.

FIFTH SUNDAY: *PRAYER*

What is Prayer? When do we pray? Are there only special times we can pray, or is God always in? Prayer is a two way communication. We need to listen as well as talk.

What do we pray for? to give thanks, praise, to pray for others including our enemies, to pray for God's presence and guidance throughout the day, not just things.

Through prayer we learn more about God and about ourselves. We learn to rely more on God and our own inner resources. We receive spiritual strength.

Pass out "Jesus Prays and Teaches Us to Pray"[1] booklets and encourage them to read through the booklet with their parents. Think about what Jesus says and teaches us about prayer.

Light fifth candle: PRAYER.

SIXTH SUNDAY: *COMMIT-MENT (Palm Sunday)*

This is a very special Sunday in Lent which is the beginning of Holy Week. Do you know what this Sunday is called? What happened on this Sunday?

As Jesus rode into Jerusalem, he was making a commitment which is a promise or a pledge to do something in the future. He was announcing to the world that he was indeed the Christ, the One sent from God. And he had made a commitment to follow God's plan all the way to the cross if necessary.

As we enter this final week of Lent think about a commitment, a promise you can make to God and to yourself to do something special for God this week. Maybe you can attend a special Maundy Thursday Service, make an Easter card or gift for a shut-in, visit someone who is lonely. We are each one God's Children, his sons and daughters; make a promise this week to act more like a child of God.

Light Sixth candle: COMMITMENT.

EASTER: *RESURRECTION SUNDAY/RENEWAL*

REPLACE ALL THE CANDLES ON THE CROSS WITH WHITE CANDLES.

Easter is a celebration of New Life, and Eternal Life that is ours because of Jesus. We remember that after he was crucified, he was buried in the tomb and on the third day he rose from the dead in a way that we don't fully understand, but we accept as true. This is the most important celebration in the church year because it illustrates that the love and the power of God are stronger than even death.

The Easter egg is a familiar symbol that reminds us of the rock that was rolled over the tomb because its hard shell looks like a rock, and it seems to have no life within. But it does contain new life which bursts out of the shell and reminds us of Jesus coming out of the tomb, and living again.

Just as God gave Jesus new life after death, and gives life to the baby chick inside the hard shell, so he can work through our hard problems and suffering to give us a new and eternal life.

Pass out Easter eggs to the Children and light the Christ Candle.

[1]*JESUS PRAYS AND TEACHES US TO PRAY*, American Bible Society, 1966.

33

LENTEN CALENDAR

by Colleen Britton

Our church was searching for a way to emphasize Lent as a period of 40 days in preparation for Easter. Why not use a Lenten calendar? Everyone was excited about the idea!

Each child was given a legal size sheet of paper which had been divided into 40 rectangles with a daily "to do" task on each square. They were also given a packet of 40 assorted Easter stickers. As each daily task was completed a sticker was placed on the rectangle.

By Easter our children had no only brightly colored calendars, but had learned more about giving, sharing, and caring for one another. They had each personally prepared for Easter.

1. Make an Easter picture for your home.

2. Help care for a pet or other animal.

3. Look for a sign of new life outside.

4. Do something extra nice for your parents.

5. Do something extra nice for a neighbor.

6. Write a letter to a grandparent.

7. Tell someone you love them.

8. Help a friend.

9. Make an Easter basket.

10. Pray the Lord s Prayer.

11. Make an Easter present for someone.

12. Make someone laugh.

13. Find a butterfly.

14. Give someone a smile.

15. Let someone else have their way.

16. Find a rainbow and remember God's promise.

17. Light a candle--think about Jesus, the light of the world.

18. Hold someone's hand.

19. What happened on Maundy Thursday? Read Luke 22:7-20.

20. Make and send an Easter card.

21. Say "thank you" to someone.

22. Pick a flower and give it to someone.

23. What happened on Palm Sunday? Read John 12:12-16.

24. Help someone clean up.

25. Decorate an Easter egg.

26. Say grace at dinner.

27. Plant a seed.

28. Share someting with a brother, sister or friend.

29. Read Matthew 5:14 16.

30. Give up something to make someone happy.

31. Help your Dad with a job.

32. Pray for someone you love.

33. Watch the sunrise. Help make it a happy day.

34. Water a plant to help it grow.

35. Read John 8:12.

36. Help Mom with a job.

37. Carry a burden for someone.

38. Pray for a joyous Easter.

39. Help someone you do not know.

40. Visit a friend.

In this service we move from light to darkness. You will need thirteen candles (one for Jesus Christ and the others from the twelve disciples). The unlighted candles should be placed in a central spot in the sanctuary or worship area. It is noted when the center Christ candle should be lit. The candles representing the disciples are to be lighted in order of the narrative following the section titled THE CALLING OF THE APOSTLES. In order, the apostles will come forward, light their candle, and then offer a brief biographical statement.

They will return to put out their candles in order in the narrative section titled THE FALLING AWAY OF THE APOSTLES. They will come forward in order, put their candle out, and then kneel at some appropriate place such as the altar or communion rail. They will remain kneeling until they go forward to pick up and carry out the cross (at the end of service at point of CROSS RECESSIONAL). The person taking the part of Judas, will put his candle out and then leave the sanctuary.

At the CROSS RECESSIONAL, the apostles will carry out the cross in silence. The worship leaders and the congregation will follow in silence. It is suggested that the cross be carried outside, and everyone pass by in silence.

THE TESTIMONY OF THE APOSTLES

PETER

I portray Peter, a quick tempered and impulsive apostle. I talked a lot and sometimes brought on trouble when I was too sure of myself. Credit has been given to me for perceiving that Jesus was indeed the Messiah, a decision arrived at by asking many questions. Jesus saw great potential in me, and visualized me as a natural leader of the Church. My road to faith was rocky, and I regret very much that I denied him. However, Christ believed that I was able; he believes that all of us are able, even when we think we aren't.

GOOD FRIDAY TENEBRAE SERVICE

by Dr. Wesley Taylor

ANDREW

I symbolize Andrew, the brother of Peter. I am known as a friendly fisherman who was always leading people to meet Christ. One of the great thrills of my life came when I introduced Peter to Jesus. Some think of me as the first foreign missionary, since I brought a group of non-Jews—Greeks—to meet the Master. The young lad with the loaves and fish also came to Jesus through my invitation. Christ gave me the courage to meet strangers and to bring them into contact with him.

JAMES

I represent James, one of the apostles in the inner circle of Jesus' friends, along with my brother John. Our father was Zebedee, the fisherman. I am an ambitious, temperamental person who sought power for myself. Nevertheless, Jesus knew that he could use me, and that my strong temperament could be channeled in a productive direction. After the Christ took charge of

35

my life, he was able to re-cycle my life for his purpose and mission.

JOHN

I depict John, the brother of James. I am thought of by many as a "son of thunder", because of my quick response in shaking my fist at those who have not been receptive to Jesus and his message. I suppose I have been intolerant at times, such as the occasion when I stopped a stranger from healing in the name of Jesus. And yet I have always remained close to the Christ, and he once referred to me as "the beloved disciple."When I think how Christ changed me from a "son of thunder" into a man of love, I realize that he can truly change the life of any man who will permit him to do so.

MATTHEW

I portray Matthew, a typical tax-gatherer of the time of Jesus, but one who was despised because of my vocation. One who collected the taxes for Rome was usually thought of as being greedy and unjust; this was because he could levy as much tax as he thought the person could pay. Because of this hatred I was sometimes even barred from attending worship. However, Jesus saw great possibilities in me, and when he invited me to follow him I quickly accepted. My original name was Levi, but Jesus gave me the new name of Matthew, which means "gift of God". My life is a testimony to the manner in which Christ can make a hated man into a blessed gift of God.

BARTHOLOMEW

I symbolize Bartholomew, who was also known as Nathanael. The first time I saw Jesus he paid me a nice compliment as he said, "Here is an Israelite; there is nothing false in him." I quickly recognized him because of his sincerity and said,"Teacher, you are the Son of God! You are the King of Israel!" I grew to appreciate the fact that Christ knows us as we really are, and

knows the depth of our sincerity in our worship and allegiance to him.

JUDAS ISCARIOT

I represent Judas, who was the treasurer of the group of twelve. Some have thought of me as a violent revolutionary because I wanted to help overthrow the Roman rulers. When Jesus failed to lead, or even join in this cause, I decided to betray him, hoping to force his hand. However, my plot failed and I was filled with remorse since I actually betrayed him into the hands of his enemies who crucified him. While you will remember me most for my betrayal, I hope that you might also learn from my life that Christ cannot be forced to do that which you desire since his way is higher and greater than that of men.

PHILIP

I depict Philip, who was the first apostle Jesus called to follow him. I introduced Nathanael to Jesus and helped Andrew to bring certain Greeks to meet him. Even though I was quiet and shy, I seemed to ask the pertinent questions at the right time. So it was that I asked Jesus to show the Greeks the Heavenly Father. This gave him the opportunity to tell them that God was at work in himself in a very special way. Christ can reveal himself to others as we open the doors and prepare the way for him to do so.

SIMON THE ZEALOT

I portray Simon, and was a member of the Zealots. This was a group of fanatical Jewish patriots who advocated revolutionary tactics to overthrow the Romans. I was disappointed when I discovered that Jesus would not become a part of this movement. However, after listening to him, and living with him, I began to realize that greater things can be accomplished through love. Christ can lead men from the ways of force and power to the way of sacrificial love.

JAMES, SON OF ALPHAEUS

I symbolize James, the son of Alphaeus. I was also an adversary of Rome, but did not express my feelings through violence. I was related to Matthew, although we differed widely on many issues. Jesus was able to bring us together, from our different viewpoints, and was able to challenge us to work together for his kingdom. Christ can reconcile men and guide them into cooperative endeavors for his Church.

THOMAS

I represent Thomas, most often referred to as the doubter. I was ready to go with Jesus anywhere. Once, when he indicated that he was going to Jerusalem, I said to the others, "Let us also go that we might die with him." I often asked searching questions, such as, "How can we know the way?" I was so stunned when he was taken away from us, that I went off alone to mourn and ponder. My mind was filled with doubt when I heard that he had returned, but I believed completely when I was able to touch his body. Christ can take away our fears and doubts as we confront him honestly, and permit him to reveal himself completely to us.

THADDAEUS

I depict Thaddaeus, and was also known as the son of James. I was always curious about many things and asked many questions. One day I asked Jesus why he had revealed himself to the twelve first, and not to the whole world. Through his answer he indicated that he only disclosed himself to loving and obedient hearts. I appreciated his answer but felt that everyone should be able to accept him as Lord. Christ reveals himself only to those who come inquiring, and who are willing to surrender their lives to him and to follow him.

GOOD FRIDAY TENEBRAE SERVICE

INTRODUCTION TO THE SERVICE

The Tenebrae Service dates from the 6th century. It is a dramatic service to remember the death of Jesus Christ. The literal translation of the Latin word, "Tenebrae," is "shadows"; thus, the service moves from light to darkness. In the early church it was celebrated on Wednesday, Thursday, and Friday of Holy Week.

The purpose of the Tenebrae Service is to help us focus on the total impact of the darkest day in the history of Christianity, the date that Jesus died on the cross. The service is in complete contrast to Easter. The mood is what the followers of Jesus felt on that Friday long ago—shock, despair, gloom, grief and sadness. When the service ends, Jesus is dead!

THE CALL TO WORSHIP

Leader: Come to Gethsemane,
        where Jesus prayed and was betrayed.
    Come to the courts of justice, to Pilate,
        where the righteous One was found guilty.
Community: Come to the hill outside Jerusalem,
        where the innocent One suffered and died.
    Come let us bow down in awe, for what
        happened there was done for us.

Silent Reading of Hymn   **"In the Cross of Christ I Glory"**

A READING

Large rusted spikes were wedged into the post salvaged from an old fence. The post stood before a group gathered for worship —
　　How is this like Good Friday?

nails. . .pain. . .Jesus. . . wood. . .dead. . .tears. . . long ago. . .now

One word for Good Friday? dying. . .suffering. . .killing . . .hurting. . . .OUCH! Good Friday was OUCH! Good Friday was that moment when God's light went out.

SCRIPTURE SENTENCES "Christ the Light"   John 1:1-5

Christ is the light of the world! As we observe the lighted Christ candle, let us remember these words from the Gospel according to John: The true light that enlightens every person was coming into the world. He was in the world, and the world was made through him. ...There was a man sent from God, whose name was John. He came to bear witness to the light.   (Light Christ candle)

THE CALLING OF THE APOSTLES

The Gospel tells us that Jesus called 12 apostles. . . These men, are to be represented by lighted candles; Jesus spoke to them saying, "You are the light of the world. A city set on a hill cannot be hid. Nor do men light a lamp and put it under a bushel, but on a stand, and it gives light to all in the house. Let your light so shine before others, that they may see your good works and give glory to your Father in heaven."

THE LIGHTING OF THE APOSTLES' CANDLES

Jesus called SIMON PETER to be a disciple...(light candle). He called also his brother, ANDREW. "As Jesus walked by the Sea of Galilee, he saw two brothers, Simon who was called Peter, and Andrew, his brother, casting a net into the sea, for they were fishermen. And he said to them, 'Follow me, and I will make you fishers of men.' Immediately they left their nets and followed. Then Jesus called JAMES to be a disciple...He also called his brother and JOHN. 'And going from there he saw two brothers, James the son of Zebedee and John, in the boat with Zebedee, their father, mending their nets and he called them. Immediately they left the boat and their father, and followed him.' "

ANTHEM

Jesus called THOMAS to be his disciple. Jesus called MATTHEW to be a disciple. He also called JUDAS ISCARIOT. Jesus called PHILIP. Jesus called SIMON, THE ZEALOT. Jesus called JAMES, SON OF ALPHAEUS, BARTHOLOMEW, and THADDAEUS.

THE CHARGE OF THE APOSTLES
INSTRUCTIONS FOR THE FUTURE (from Matthew 10)

Jesus said to the disciples: "As you go, proclaim the message: 'The kingdom of heaven is upon you.' Heal the sick, raise the dead, cleanse lepers, cast out devils. You received without cost; give without charge...Look I send you out like sheep among wolves; be wary as serpents, innocent as doves. And be on your guard, for men will hand you over to their courts, they will flog you in the synagogues, and you will be brought before governors and kings, for my sake. But when you are arrested, do not worry about what you are to say; when the time comes, the words you need will be given you; for it is not you who will be speaking, it will be the Spirit speaking in you."

HYMN   "When I Survey the Wondrous Cross"

THE FALLING AWAY OF THE APOSTLES

When Jesus had spoken these words, he went forth with his disciples across the Kidron Valley, where there was a garden, which he and his disciples entered. Now Judas, who betrayed him, also knew the place; for Jesus often met there with his disciples. So Judas, procuring a band of soldiers and some officers from the chief priests, and the Pharisees, went there with lanterns, torches, and weapons. Then Jesus came forward and said to them, "Whom do you seek?" Judas, who betrayed him, was standing with them. When he said to them, "I am he," he drew back and fell to the ground (extinguish JUDAS candle). Again he asked them, "Whom do you seek?" and they said 'Jesus of Nazareth.' Jesus answered, "I told you that I am he."

Then Simon Peter, having a sword, drew it and struck the high priest's slave and cut off his right ear. (THOMAS) Jesus said to Peter, "Put your sword into its sheath; shall I not drink the cup which the father has given me?" So the band of soldiers and their captain and the officers of the Jews seized Jesus and bound him and led him to the high priest. Simon Peter followed Jesus, and so did another disciple. As this disciple was known to the high priest, he entered the court of the high priest along with Jesus, while Peter stood outside the door. So the other disciple went back out, spoke to the girl at the gate, and brought Peter inside. The girl at the gate said to Peter, "Aren't you also one of the disciples of that man?" "No, I am not," answered Peter. (SIMON, THE ZEALOT) It was cold, so the servants and guards had built a charcoal fire and were standing around it, warming themselves. So Peter went over and stood with them, warming himself.

ANTHEM

The high priest questioned Jesus about his disciples and about his teachings. Jesus answered, "I have always spoken publicly to everyone; all my teaching was done in the synagogues and in the Temple, where all the people come together. (MATTHEW)

Peter was still standing outside keeping himself warm. So the others said to him: "Aren't you also one of the disciples of that man?" But Peter denied it. "No, I am not," he said. One of the High Priest's slaves, a relative of the man whose ear Peter had cut off, spoke up. "Didn't I see you with him in the garden?" he asked. Again Peter said "no"--and at once a rooster crowed. (PHILIP)

Early in the morning Jesus was taken from Caiaphas' house to the governor's palace. The Jewish authorities did not go inside the palace, for they wanted to keep themselves ritually clean to eat the Passover meal. So Pilate went outside to them and asked, "What do you accuse this man of?" Their answer was: "We would not have brought him to you if he had not committed a crime." Pilate said to them, "Then you yourselves take him and try him according to your own law." They replied, "We are not allowed to put anyone to death." Pilate went back into the palace and called Jesus. "Are you king of the Jews?" he asked him.

Jesus answered, "Does this question come from you or have others told you about me?" Pilate replied, "Do you think I am a Jew? It was your own people and the chief priest who handed you over to me. What have you done?" (JOHN) Jesus said, "My kingdom does not belong to this world; if my kingdom belonged to this world, my followers would fight to keep me from being handed over to the Jewish authorities. No, my kingdom does not belong here!" Pilate said to him, "So, you are a king?" Jesus answered, "You say that I am a king." (JAMES, SON OF ALPHAEUS)

ANTHEM

Then Pilate went back outside to the people and said to them, "I cannot find any reason to condemn him, but according to the custom you have, I always set free for you a prisoner during the Passover. Do you want me to set free for you the king of the Jews? They answered him with a shout, "No, not him! We want Barabbas!" (BARTHOLOMEW) Then Pilate took Jesus and had him whipped. The soldiers made a crown out of thorny branches and put it on his head; then they put a purple robe on him and came to him and said, "Long live the king of the Jews!" And they went up and slapped him. Pilate went back out once more and said to the crowd, "Look, I will bring him out here to you to let you see that I cannot find any reason to condemn him." So Jesus came out, wearing the crown of thorns and the purple robe. When the chief priests and the temple guards saw him, they shouted, "Crucify him! Crucify him! Crucify him!" (THADDAEUS AND JAMES)

Pilate said to them, "You take him, then, and crucify him. I find no reason to condemn him." (ANDREW)

Pilate handed Jesus over to them to be crucified.

He went out, carrying his cross and came to "The Place of the Skull", as it is called. In Hebrew it is called "Golgotha". There they crucified him. Pilate wrote a notice and had it put on the cross. (PETER)

"Jesus of Nazareth, the king of the Jews", is what he wrote. Many people read it, because the place where Jesus was crucified was not far from the city. The notice was written in Hebrew, Latin, and Greek. The chief priests said to Pilate, "Do not write 'The king of the Jews', but rather, 'This man said I am the king of the Jews.' Pilate answered, "What I have written stays written."

House lights out

ANTHEM: "Were You There"

Jesus knew that by now everything had been completed; and in order to make the scripture come true, he said, "I am thirsty".

A bowl was there, full of cheap wine; so a sponge was soaked in the wine, put on a stalk of hyssop, and lifted to his lips. Jesus drank the wine and said,''It is finished!'' Then he bowed his head and died. *(Here extinguish the Christ Candle)*

narration (from off stage -- hear voice only)

This moment has fullest meaning only if we think completely about the death of Jesus and remember that this is God dying for us. It is impossible for us to really fathom what happened at Golgotha. Jesus put to death. But we know that God's redeeming work is almost done, and our salvation is purchased at the most outrageous price of death... we simply wait in the presence of our Lord's death and appropriate as much meaning as possible. Considering the affirmation of this moment:

> a perfect sacrifice has been made for my sins...
> I am loved to the uttermost...
> there is no need for defensiveness now...
> there is no reason to be lonely any longer...
> I am justified by Jesus' death—to be fully loved by God...
> loved by God as though I were sinless...
> by his death, Jesus conquered death...
> no longer do I need to fear death...
> his death is a gift, the ultimate gift of God's love...
> if I accept Jesus' gift of love in death,
> it will transform my life.

CROSS RECESSIONAL

THOSE IMPOSSIBLE EGGS

by Ida F. Killian

A devotional service for church school classes, prayer groups, women's circles, men's meetings, or intergenerational groups.

Materials needed:

A plastic egg which separates in two for each person in the group. These are inexpensive and available in a variety of colors.

A piece of 3" x 5" paper for each egg

Similiar number of pencils

The program outlined here is designed for ten participants but there is no limit to the size of the group. The women's circle in my church used a form of this devotional with about twenty in attendance.

Before the service begins a different verse of Scripture is written on each slip of paper and one is enclosed in each egg. Eggs are piled in an Easter basket and used as decoration until their part in the program.

Leader: *Read Scripture passage Luke 11:11-13. Emphasize verse 12.*

The egg has always been important especially as a symbol of new life. That is why it has particular meaning and significance during the Lenten and Easter season. Some one has called it the "impossible egg." Outwardly it seems almost impossible that a living creature could emerge from such an enclosure without access to the outside world for sustenance. But a living creature does break that shell and steps out into a vast new universe. Today at the beginning of Lent we are each going to have our own personal impossible egg.

(The basket is passed around and each member is invited to select an egg.)

It is quite certain that everyone here has some secret wish or deep sincere desire for himself or another which seems almost impossible to attain. With prayer and dedication your egg can be a daily reminder that God can do the impossible. Let Him speak to you through your egg from now until Easter.

Prayer: Our Father, we know every good and perfect gift comes from You. Help us to ask in faith believing You will answer as we pray in the name of Jesus Christ. Amen.

As we open our eggs one by one each person will read aloud the verse he finds inside.

Suggested verses are:

Luke 11:9	Gal. 3:22
Matt. 19:26	Luke 1:37
Mark 9:23	Heb. 11:6
Matt. 8:13	Prov. 23:7
John 20:31	Eph. 3:20

Now turn your paper over and write on the back your sincere desire, your seemingly impossible dream. Fold the paper, put it back into the egg and join the shells together again. Take the egg home and put it on your table or some other prominent place where you will see it every day. Do not open it again until Easter. Allow it to incubate. Repeat your verse daily. Let prayer nurture your desire until it becomes the substance of things hoped for and evidence in tangible form.

Prayer: Father we go in faith. As Jesus emerged from the ttomb may our hidden desires find new life. As living creatures break forth from confining shells may we see our requests become reality. In Jesus' name we pray. Amen.

Note: Since many of these are very personal requests no one is asked later to reveal results but any who wish might tell of answered prayer, new insight or closer relationship with their Lord through this daily communion. It is hoped these little eggs might be a symbol of more vital Christian living and a graphic suggestion for praying more effectively.

THINKING CHRISTIANLY ABOUT LENT

by Rudy H. Thomas

Some thirty-four years ago a book was published in which the author, on the very first page, declares:

> If to think Christianly means anything, it means to think differently from the usual forms of thinking. It means to consider all the problems of life in a perspective quite different from the conventional perspectives. To do this is hard – far harder than most of us realize, for most of us are so completely and usually unconsciously absorbed in the conventional values and patterns of twentieth-century western civilization that even when we try to think Christianly we are actually thinking conventionally.

Thinking Christianly
by W. Burnet Easton

The more I thought of it the more it bore into my consciousness that we who call ourselves Christians so often DO NOT THINK CHRISTIANLY. What we do is think *conventionally* and then add a few pious phrases and biblical quotations to make the thinking appear Christian.

What then shall we say and think about Lent? One of the first things that comes to many peoples' minds when they think of Lent is this business of giving up

something, denying yourself something you usually enjoy. There is subtle temptation here that leads to self-deception if we are not very careful. I think of the junior high school girl who was asked what she was giving up for Lent and she said she narrowed it down to one of two things — either lipstick or pizza; then she piously announced her decision. She would give up pizza. Her self-deception was unmasked when a friend asked her, "Do you really like pizza?" "Heavens no," she replied, "I hate it!"

Well, this business of giving up something during Lent needs careful scrutiny. Frankly, I have never given up anything, particularly during Lent. I always felt if there was something I ought to give up during Lent, then I ought to give it up the rest of the year too. I believe this matter of giving up something involves some very mixed up motives. I suspect that many a person who gives up coke, beer, or candy during Lent is really more calorie-conscious than Christ-conscious.

I would suggest that if we limit our thinking regarding Lent to a matter of giving up something then we limit the spiritual impact of this season upon our lives. Rather than think so much in terms of giving up something, I prefer to think in terms of giving ourselves more fully to *something*! The emphasis should be more on the doing of something positive than the elimination of something negative.

43

I recall a young people's group in a church that discussed the question of what to give up during Lent and they decided they would not give up anything particularly but they would give themselves more fully to something worthwhile. As they talked of what would be truly a worthy "sacrifice" they decided the usual ones of candy, movies, or coke seemed really petty, so instead they upped the tithes from 10% to 20%, gave blood to the bloodmobile, and pledged hours of help to families who had illness. They said, "We'll go to the movies if we have time. We will eat candy and cake because they are not very precious. But we'll give things that really matter — time, blood, money, and energy."

A brief word about fasting, another traditional religious practice for some, is appropriate. In the apocryphal writing, "The Sheperd of Hermas," there is a very interesting dialogue that takes place on the subject of fasting.

As I fasted and sat upon a certain mountain and was thanking the Lord for all the things He had wrought with me, I saw the Shepherd sitting by men and saying, "Why art thou come hither thus early?"

"Because, Sir," quoth I, "I am keeping a station. I am fasting."

"What fast is this that ye fast?" said the Shepherd, "Ye know not how to fast unto the Lord, neither is this unprofitable fasting unto Him a fast, but I will tell thee what is a full fast and one acceptable unto the Lord. Fast thou such a fast as this unto God. Do no wickedness in thy life, and serve the Lord with a pure heart. Keep His precepts and walk in His ordinances, and let no evil lust arise in thy heart. Believe in God. If thou do these things, thou shalt accomplish a great fast and one acceptable to God."

So, traditional fasting also has its dangers. When we practice a religious rite we are always in danger of thinking that in the rite lies our salvation. It may indeed be profitable for a person's soul or body to deny themselves certain things during Lent. I find no fault with that. It may be well for a person to fast. These things may be well and good providing we always do them with honesty knowing that God knows the real motivations of our hearts.

If we think Christianly about Lent we will take a good long look at all the blessings we have known from a provident God. I recall reading of a London scrubwoman who became ill. She was very poor and her friends pooled their resources and sent her to the hospital. During her convalescence she visited other patients up and down the hall. Across the hall from her room was a twelve year old boy who was critically ill. The old lady and young boy would talk for long periods each day.

Early one morning the scrubwoman was awakened by the boy's mother who said, "The doctors say Johnny has about ten minutes to live. Won't you say something to him?"

That was no easy assignment as I well know, but that little old lady, with courage and the faith of a saint, walked into that room and sat beside the dying boy. She took his thin hands between her calloused palms and said to him, "Listen, Johnny, God *made you.* God *loves you.* God sent His Son to *save you.* God wants you to come home to *live with Him.*"

The little boy propped himself up on his elbow and with a feeble voice said, "Say it again - say it again!" Quietly the old lady said, "God *made you,* Johnny, and God *loves you.* God sent His Son to *save you.* God wants you to come home to *live with Him.*"

Johnny looked into the kindly face of his friend, and said, "Tell God, *thank you!*"

Lent is a time to tell God "Thank You."

44

Youth Activities

FROM PALM SUNDAY TO. . .

by Robert G. Davidson

We see the joyful entry of a celebrated man into the great city and share the excitement this event brings to the people. But, as events unfold during the coming days we see misunderstandings, separation, deep hurt and pain. How would you have responded and reacted if you had been there that Palm Sunday and the immediate following days?

During this program there will be time to identify the events which took place during this historical week; the relationships between significant persons; the joyful moments and the periods of deep despair. There should also be time for members of the group to meditate upon these experiences and see if they might identify with these happenings.

Begin the program by having the group form small conversation/study groups and assign one of the following situations to each group. Ask each group to create a role play of its situation to share with the larger group. Then using the questions presented as a spring board, create a continuing story for the situation being as creative as possible in developing the story. The large group can discuss the situation after each presentation sorting through the feelings and emotions encountered and experienced.

1. The joyful celebration as Jesus enters Jerusalem on Palm Sunday. Why was the crowd so excited and filled with so much joy? Have you ever experienced overwhelming excitement as part of a large crowd? What were your feelings and how did you express them? How did the disciples feel on this day as they walked into Jerusalem with Jesus? Were they filled with joy because the crowds were honoring Jesus and were they being honored also? Did they have hopes that Jesus would soon become a great leader of the people of Israel? Have you ever experienced hope and joy for one significant person?

2. The twelve disciples and others were gathered around a table that night to share what would become the Last Supper. What were the feelings shared that night? Have you ever experienced a feeling of celebration as you sat around a table with friends? What were the feelings of the disciples as Judas left the group? Was there a feeling of breaking apart a community of friends? Have you ever experienced this? In what type of situation? How was it resolved or was it?

3. The tangled emotions and feelings of Judas, a man who was a loyal and trusted member of the disciples who gathered about Jesus. Judas listened to Jesus as he taught and asked questions and was deeply influenced by Jesus. He had great expectations for Jesus as he entered Jerusalem — Jesus would lead the people of Israel to freedom, freedom from Roman control. But in the days after Palm Sunday Jesus made no move to lead the people to freedom of which Judas had dreamed. How might Judas force Jesus into action? Have you ever tried to force anyone into action? Did Judas betray Jesus in an attempt to force Jesus to become a political leader? Did this cause only complete separation from Jesus? How do think Judas felt at this point? What kind of despair was he experiencing?

4. The night after Jesus had been taken prisoner, the most loyal and closest friend of Jesus denied knowing him three times — the man Peter who went on to become one of the greatest leaders of the early church. Why did Peter deny knowing Jesus that night — deep fear? How do you think Peter felt doing this? Have

you ever turned against a friend because other people did? How did you feel? What is the feeling of separation from a trusted friend?

5. It is Friday and a crucifixion has taken place. You have been standing in the distance watching the events of the day — the crowd of screaming and yelling people following the prisoner to the hill, the quietness which fell over the crowd as the cross rose up and then settled into its hole in the ground, and the wonder which came across the faces in the crowd as Jesus spoke his final words from the cross. And then, the complete silence which fell across everything. What are the feelings of hopelessness and despair — the complete separation being experienced here in this event? Are there situations like them, maybe on a lesser scale, which we experience today?

JESUS WAS CRUCIFIED

by Jane Landreth

This puzzle contains information about Jesus' crucifixion. To work the puzzle you will need this code:

A 1, B 2, C 3, D 4, E 5, F 6, G 7, H 8, I 9, J 10, K 11, L 12, M 13, N 14, O 15, P 16, Q 17, R 18, S 19, T 20, U 21, V 22, W 23, X 24, Y 25, Z 26

Read each clue. Fill in the coded word.

1. Jesus was brought to trial before 16—9—12—1—20—5.

2. At his crucifixion, Jesus was mocked by the chief priests, 19—3—18—9—2—5—19, and elders.

3. Jesus was crucified beside two 20—8—9—5—22—5—19.

4. Golgotha was also called the place of the 19—11—21—12—12.

5. The 19—15—12—4—9—5—18—19 cast losts for Jesus' garments.

6. Someone offered Jesus a sponge filled with 22—9—14—5—7—1—18 to drink.

7. A sign that said, "Jesus, 11—9—14—7 of the Jews, was nailed above Jesus' head.

8. The people said to Jesus, "If you are the Son of God, come down from th3—18—15—19—19."

9. From the sixth hour a 4—1—18—11—14—5—19—19 fell over the land.

10. Jesus was taken down from the cross and laid in a 20—15—13—2.

THE STORY OF LENT

by Elaine M. Ward

The climax of the Christian year is the season of Easter. God's story of revelation was **introduced** at Christmas with the birth of a baby, Jesus of Nazareth.

We listen to the **plot** of God's story, as we hear stories about Jesus and Jesus' stories. The happenings, the **action** of God's story, leads to the **climax** of the story, the struggle, betrayal, crucifixion, death, and resurrection of Jesus the Christ.

The **end** of the story is the beginning of the Christian church, people who heard Jesus' parables and saw Jesus as a parable, the Parable of God, God revealed.

All stories have these four parts and so the story is recorded in the Bible, and yet the story as each individual encounters it is more than what is written, more than what actually happened, as important and crucial as this is to our understanding. It is more, because it is what God, through the story, speaks to me, to you, as we listen and learn about ourselves in relation to God and our neighbor, in dialogue with God and our neighbor.

As I hear or read the story of that desolate, lonely night in the Garden of Gethsemane in prayer, the words of Jesus, "Remove this cup from me," I encounter my own fear.

As I hear or read Jesus' words to his friends, "One of you shall betray me this night," I recognize my own betrayal and ask with them, "Is it I?"

As I hear or read Peter's denial, "I know him not!" I encounter my own doubt, my own denial.

As I hear or read Pilate's words, "I wash my hands," I face my own complacency, my own lack of total involvement, responsibility, commitment.

As I hear and read of the crucifixion and death, I am there watching, waiting, silently watching, a spectator rather than a participant.

As I hear and read of the resurrection, I am faced with the women's fears and hesitation, with Thomas' doubt, with the disciples' discouragement that I, too, have faced.

As Jacob struggled with the angel until he received the blessing, we must struggle with the story, with God's word, until we hear God speak to us.

As we dialog with and encounter the word, it becomes more than great religious literature, sacred history, dramatic biography, vision, confession, or prayer.

As we dialog with and encounter the Easter story, it is God speaking to you and me through the story to our own unique situations here and now.

As we identify with the story, it becomes our story, the story that shapes what we see and hear and do.

Lent is the most fitting season of the church year to encounter God's word, God's will and purpose, and God's ultimate salvation, as one dialogues with his word in the story.

Nikos Kazantzakis' story of St. Francis is an example of encountering the Easter story: "Listen, my child," he said, "each year at Easter I used to watch Christ's resurrection. All the faithful would gather around his tomb and weep, weep inconsolably, beating on the ground to make it open. And behold! In the midst of our lamentations the tombstone crumbled to pieces and Christ sprang from the earth and ascended to heaven, smiling at us and waving a white banner. There was only one year I did not see Him resurrected. That year a theologican of consequence, a graduate of the University of Bologna, came to us. He mounted the pulpit in church and began to elucidate the resurrection for hours on end. He explained and explained until our heads began to swim; and that year the tombstone did not crumble, and, I swear to you, no one saw the resurrection."

Experience, not history, proves a story true, for stories are symbols of inner realities, of experiences in the deeper recesses of the person.

The following story, based on a story by Robert McAfee Brown, relates one man's encounter with the Easter story, the message of resurrection.

THE MIRACLE OF RESURRECTION
(A true story based on John 11:25-26)

The small group of Marines closed their Bibles. Having read the story of Jesus raising Lazarus from the dead, they leaned back in their chairs with their private thoughts. Different feelings crowded their minds.

"I can't **buy** that story. Dead is dead. I sure know that!" one of the marines thought, as he listened to the story being discussed. The 1,500 marines who were coming home from war in Japan knew in a very real way what death was.

"I wonder if it really happened? Oh, well, even if it did then, it doesn't involve me today!" The young marine yawned and smiled sheepishly at the chaplain. "The important thing is that I'll be home tomorrow!"

"That story dramatized Jesus' words. What a teacher! I can hardly wait to get back to the classroom," thought the middle-aged marine, patting his Bible gently. How he loved the feel and the smell of books!

One of the marines sat taunt in his chair. He gripped his Bible and breathed heavily. It was as if he were alone in that group of men. "It can't be!" thought the young man. "Though he were dead, yet shall he live! Jesus seems to be talking to me, to ME!"

The Bible study closed with prayer and the men returned to their cabins. The chaplain gathered his books, wondering if anyone had understood at all. Whether Lazarus came back to life two thousand years ago was not as important as whether Jesus' words, his promise of "new life," were true today. I wonder how many of us know that we are dead to God, to real life in Christ, while we still walk and move and breathe? The chaplain shook his head. It wasn't easy being a messenger of God. It was difficult being a chaplain to marines. He wondered if it would be any easier being a pastor back home?

The chaplain turned to close his cabin door, deep in his own thoughts about the future, now that the war was over. "Hello?" he spoke with surprise.

The young marine at the door stammered, "I . . thought . . I need . . do you have time to . ."

"Sit down." The chaplain put the young man at ease and soon the corporal was telling his story. "I had just finished high school when I went into the service and was immediately sent to Japan. The war was hell. I was scared. Then, without knowing it, I got used to it, and became bored with it all. One night some friends and I got into trouble..bad trouble. Luckily no one knew about it."

The young man bit his lip. "Well, that is, I knew about it . . and . . God knew about it! I couldn't forgive myself. I felt terribly guilty. I had ruined my life and my family would never . . I . ."

50

The chaplain poured a glass of water and the corporal gulped down the water, glad for a moment to stop. Then he continued. "I felt dead. I've been dead, but now, reading about Jesus and Lazarus, I suddenly knew that I was alive again. God had forgiven me. The resurrection of Lazarus was happening to me. It was real. It was now. It was me."

Together they talked about what the corporal would do to "correct" his mistake. "It won't be easy.." he admitted slowly, and taking a deep breath, he added with a smile, "but now I am **living**!"

The miracle of resurrection had taken place on a Navy transport ship in the middle of the Pacific Ocean. It took place in 1946. It would continue to happen as long as the words of Jesus were read. The miracle of resurrection is true..today!

The Easter story reminds each of us of God's grace, of the drama of God's love, and of the joy of God's "good news."

Our stories are the foundation of our faith, the resurrection of our hope, as we pilgrimage toward the light, the light of Easter Sunday. Such stories are a compass for our way, for they help us walk in mercy and live in mystery, rejoicing in the majesty of Our Maker, the One who Resurrects.

PROGRAM ACTIVITIES:

1. Read Psalm 148 aloud. Ask each participant to choose one thing for which he can praise. With fingerpaint, tempera, felt-tipped markers, water colors, or crayons invite participants to illustrate their "praise". Take slides of the finished work and when the slides are being shown, read Psalm 148.

2. In small groups make flying kites. You will need two sticks that are light and flat or buy balsa wood from a hobby shop, measuring 20" long, 3/8" wide, 1/8" thick. Make notches on both sides of the sticks 1" from the tip. Have 3 yards of string for the tail.

Place one stick on top of the other, calling attention to the "cross." Glue at the center joint. Wind string around the center for strength. Tie string from the ball of string around the notch of one stick, pull the string to the next notch and tie. Continue going from notch to notch until you are where you started. Tie and cut the string.

Cut a piece of tissue paper 20" x 20" and cut 2" from each corner. Paint a butterfly onto the tissue with tempera paints. Cover "spots" on the butterfly with white glue, sprinkling glitter onto the glue. Write the words "Christ Is Risen!" Place the frame in the middle of the paper. Fold 2" of each paper edge over the strings and glue.

Tie a string 12" long to the end of each stick, gather the strings to make a tent. Tie these four strings to the ball of string, which is the kite line. Tie narrow strips of cloth 6" apart on the kite tail.

3. List "feeling" words associated with Lent, such as: Good Friday, betrayal, truth, cross, suffering, salvation, resurrection, Easter, faith. In groups of three talk about your feelings and your faith. Is yours a Good Friday or an Easter Sunday faith? Explain.

4. How are we God's stories? Have you ever experienced "encountering" God? Can you put it into words? Have you ever dialogued with God? Discuss.

5. Draw a cross and ask each individual to outline his/her hands, cut them out, write something they will do during Lent for someone else, and glue or attach them to the cross as a reminder of the importance of hands.

6. Ask each participant to draw a large egg on a piece of 9 x 12" pastel color construction paper, and draw a symbol of Easter, or words symbolic of Easter, such as love, hope, joy, rebirth, etc., incorporating their name into the words or design. Talk about the "eggs" and the designs, the transformation Easter brings with new life in nature and the spirit, and pass the eggs so that each person can write a "hope" or blessing about the person whose name is on the egg, a blessing they hope will "hatch." Return the eggs to their owners to read in silence and pray together for one another's new life in Christ.

JESUS IS ALIVE!

by Jane Landreth

Jesus appeared to the disciples following his resurrection. Find out about his appearance. Choose the best answer for each sentence. Read Luke 24:36-53 to check your answers.

1. Jesus appeared to the disciples and said,
   a. stop b. peace c. hello

2. The disciples were
   a. frightened b. asleep c. angry

3. Jesus showed the disciples his
   a. hair b. clothes c. hands and feet

4. Jesus sat down and
   a. ate with them b. slept with them c. sang with them

5. Jesus helped the disciples understand
   a. the soldiers b. their fears c. the Scriptures

6. Jesus rose from the dead on the
   a. first day b. third day c. seventh day

7. The disciples preached the good news starting at
   a. Nazareth b. Bethlehem c. Jerusalem

8. The disciples were told to wait in Jerusalem for
   a. Bibles b. God's power c. new friends

9. Jesus left the disciples and went
   a. to Heaven b. down the road c. to the temple

10. The disciples continued to
    a. sleep b. walk along the road c. praise God

Answers: 1. b, 2. a, 3. c, 4. a, 5. c, 6. b, 7. c, 8. b, 9. a, 10. c

THE NIGHT JESUS WAS ARRESTED

by Benjamin Blodget

Youth enjoy drama and surprises. For a special event during Lent, plan a service taking the youth group back in time to the arrest of Jesus.

The setting can be in the cellar of an old house or in the church basement decorated to look like underground catacombs. We were fortunate enough to have a house with granite foundation which had been whitewashed sometime in the distant past. Burlap or other drapery can be used to section off the part of the cellar to be used. If it is cold and damp, so much the better. Candles can provide light, and a charcoal brazier can be burning for heat. Add anything that will enhance the atmosphere of the Eastern Mediterranean area.

To add mystery, the youth group is told nothing except to appear outside of the designated place after it is completely dark. The leader meets the group on the street and instructs them to be completely quiet. Hand in hand, the group is guided silently through the dark building to the dimly lit "catacombs."

When all are seated on the floor, the leader can begin:

"We should be quite safe here, but there is unrest in the streets and Roman soldiers are all over the city. Now, followers of Jesus, I have some sad news. Jesus has been arrested. They have taken him away. He was up in the Garden of Gethsemane with some of his disciples... Andrew, you were there. Tell us what happened."

The leader opens the Bible and passes it to "Andrew." A card gives him written instructions to "Read Matthew 26:47-50." (Be sure to have a candle for the reader to use.)

Leader (taking the Bible back): "So now... all that we dreamed of... of a heavenly kingdom with Jesus on the throne is finished. What hope have we now? Just think, three years gone for nothing. It will be hard to go back to our villages and pick up our former lives again. But he surely brought this on himself. We tried to warn him that it was not safe to come here for Passover. Rebecca, you remember what he did when we first came to Jerusalem... how he angered the chief priests and scribes."

The open Bible is passed to

"Rebecca" with a card instructing her to read Mark 11:15-19.

Leader (passing the Bible next to Timothy): "And 'Timothy,' you were there when the Pharisees tried to trap Jesus. What happened then?"

"Timothy" reads Mark 12:13-17.

Leader: "Yes, Jesus did some strange things all right. I still don't understand some of them. Like the time he praised that woman at Simon's house. How embarrassed we men were when he defended her. It was unbelievable the way she came right in and spoke to Jesus the same as a man would. She should have stayed out in the kitchen with the other women. Lydia... you were there and heard it all..." Lydia is passed the Bible with an instruction card to read Matthew 26:6-13.

Leader: "It almost sounded as if he knew he were going to die. And the disciples who ate the Passover meal with him last night mentioned this feeling too. You felt it, didn't you, Andrew?"

"Andrew" is passed the Bible with an instruction card to

read Matthew 26:26-29.

Leader: "If we could only believe that Jesus would see us again as he said... but he is gone and doesn't seem to care about saving himself or us. Here we are in hiding... afraid. I can only think of the words of the 22nd Psalm (read Psalm 22:1-5). Maybe something will happen, if we hope, if we believe, just as our Hebrew forefathers did. And we must never forget how warm and happy and close we were when we were with Jesus.

"Now you hunger and thirst. Let us refresh ourselves before we steal out into the city streets and go back to our homes."

Take a flat Syrian bread and pass it around the circle so that each person can tear off a piece. Have a bowl of dip and a bowl of fruit. We also had a pan of spiced chicken livers to be eaten with tooth picks. A hot drink can be prepared beforehand and kept warm on the brazier.

The dialogue can be lengthened by adding more passages of scripture or making up a few lines of poetry following each reading. However, the above seemed a good length for the interest span of our group, which was quite impressed with the event.

ABBA FATHER

by Marlene Bagnull

What was Jesus feeling on Palm Sunday?

He knew that the multitudes who on that day had shouted "Hosanna" would by the end of the week shout, "crucify him." He knew that one from his inner circle of followers would betray him and that one of his closest friends would deny even knowing him. He knew that although he was God's son, he would not be spared any of the pain and anguish of dying on the cross.

What might have been Jesus' prayer that evening?

Although no one can know what our Lord may have prayed, the scriptures tell us that Jesus "understands our weaknesses, since he had the same temptations that we do" (Hebrew 4:15).

For Jesus, certainly the road to the cross was not an easy one to walk, nor are the roads that we walk today as his followers. However, through seeking the attitude of Christ, especially toward adversity, we will be drawn closer to him and enabled to negotiate the problems and hurts that are a part of following in the footsteps of Jesus.

What did Jesus pray on Palm Sunday evening? Perhaps he said,

Abba Father,
  I cannot sleep.
I'm exhausted from the events of this long and
  difficult day, yet my inner turmoil keeps
  me awake.
Another step in the fulfillment of the scriptures
  was accomplished today as I rode into
  Jerusalem on the back of that young and
  gentle donkey.
Oh Father, comfort and sustain me
  as each day brings me closer to the cross.
Please let me feel you near me.
Please fill me with your strength so that I do
  not turn back from this path that I willingly
  chose to follow so long ago.

Today my heart felt crushed - broken - within me
  as I viewed Jerusalem, as I thought of how
  ardently they have prayed for the Messiah.
Yet how blind they have been to recognize that
  I have come, and what a price will be
  paid for their rejection of me.

Oh Father, how I yearn to spare them the
  destruction that surely is to come.
If only they could see beyond the liberation of
  Israel, to the liberation that no man can take
  from another- to the liberation of man's
  souls- that liberation from the power
  of sin and death, that liberation which
  will be accomplished so very soon
  through my very life's blood.

Please give me the faith to keep believing
that I have sown seeds that will bear fruit.
How discouraged I feel when even my disciples
do not understand the purpose for my coming.
Please give me the patience to keep teaching -
keep explaining - that which I had hoped would
be so clear to them before now.
Help me to not become disheartened and
frustrated with them.
And let me not forget to be sensitive to their
feelings of utter dismay and confusion that
I know my words of sacrifice and death
bring to them.
Help me to gently show them that this is the way -
your way, the way by which all men will
be able to be made right with you.

I'm so tired. I must rest.
I must replenish the resources of the flesh
in preparation for all that lies ahead.
Father, for the thoughts and feelings
that keep racing through my mind:
my awareness of the fickleness and
insincerity of the crowds who today
would crown me king, yet by the end of
the week will shout "Crucify"; the anger and the
indignation I felt as I saw your house
of prayer turned into a market-place
to fatten men's purses at the price
of robbing the poor who come to worship;
the needs, that would consume me, of the
blind and crippled who again came to me for
healing; the confusion and concern
and anxiety and even doubt I saw in
the eyes of the disciples; and the pain
that stabs at me deep within, as each day
brings them closer to the cross...

Father, for all these feelings I need your
spirit's calming of my inner self.
Please envelop me with your presence.
Please help me to again hear your voice
encouraging me and strengthening me,
and most especially filling me with your peace;
that I might rest - rest and be renewed in you,
Father - you are my hope, my confidence,
and my unfailing strength.

SUGGESTIONS FOR GROUP USE

Read together the introduction to "Abba Father", stopping to discuss the questions that are raised. Then, as one member of your group reads Jesus' prayer, close your eyes and think how you would feel, and what you would have prayed, if you had been Jesus. You may decide to have the reader stop at points to discuss an aspect of this imaginary prayer. Share your thoughts and feelings with one another.

1. Do you agree or disagree with what the author thinks that Jesus might have prayed? Why or why not?

2. What do *you* think Jesus might have prayed?

3. What difference does thinking about Jesus' prayer make in terms of your own personal prayer life?

4. Do you think that in your prayers you are as free as Jesus was to bring his problems and needs to God in prayer? Why or why not?

5. What difference has praying made when you were faced with a "cross"?

Beyond sharing with one another, you may want to talk to your pastor about the possibility of sharing your discoveries with your congregation in the Palm Sunday morning or evening worship service. Someone from your group could read the prayer as it is printed, with several others volunteering to respond with a summation of the group's feelings about Jesus' prayer as he faced the cross, and what difference this makes to them as they face difficult things today.

(Reference: Matthew 21:1-14 and Luke 19:28-46)

THE SYMBOL OF THE CROSS:
The Secret in His Dying

by Elaine M. Ward

Throughout the history of Christianity the symbol of the cross has been its center. It is the cross that reminds us of Christ, our Lord, of our faith and salvation, of our commitment to love, even to the giving of one's life, and to the removal of the heaviness of our burdens, replaced by the acceptance of love and joy in his service.

In **Pilgrim's Progress,** Paul Bunyan describes Christian's movements on the way of his pilgrimage. Inching along beneath his burden, Christian confronts the cross, seeing below it, the sepulcher. Bunyan describes it:

"Just as Christian came up with the cross his burden loosened from off his shoulders and fell from his back and began to tumble, and so continued to do, till it came to the mouth of the sepulcher, where it fell in and I saw it no more.

"Then was Christian glad and lightsome, and said with a merry heart, 'He hath given me rest by His sorrow and life by His death.' Then he stood a while to look and wonder; FOR IT WAS SURPRISING TO HIM THAT THE SIGHT OF THE CROSS SHOULD THUS EASE HIM OF HIS BURDEN."

Symbols and metaphors are the language of the imagination, the key to faith, the language of experiences too deep and demanding to be expressed in any other way, experiences that transcend reality, truth that is filled with mystery. We are symbol makers. Made "in the image of God," we create symbols to express what we believe and perform in ritual. Easter is the symbol of rebirth in the resurrection of Christ.

Stories are such symbols. The story of the crucifixion, the story of Christ's resurrection, have a power because of their symbolic, spiritual, meaning. There is a truth and wisdom, a strength and vision, that is available through the story.

James Carroll tells us such a story in his "Secret In His Dying."[1]

Once upon a time... a fierce dragon frightened everyone in the realm. No one went out at night, every lock was bolted by day, no one traveled nor worked, and the king was perplexed.

"The farmers will not farm. The children will not learn. The traders will not trade. Even the robbers will not rob," said the king.

"At least the ruler must rule," said an old lord. So at last the king decided that an army would be raised from the people to rid the realm of the dragon, and so it was. Every male subject was required to report immediately. Everyone did.. but one young

57

man who wrote a courteous letter to the king, explaining that he must decline because he was a peaceable man and could kill no living thing.

"So am I," said the king, when he had the man brought to him, "but peace in our realm requires us to bear arms against the evil dragon."

The king knew that such a refusal, if widespread, would make his army impossible and commanded the young man's head chopped off.

The war went on and on until the whole realm was devasted by the fighting. The dragon was never found. The king grew very old and discovered that wars are easier begun than finished.

At last someone suggested they speak to the fairy by the stream, the lady of wisdom, and they gathered at her cave, seeking the secret for stopping the wars. "I have given that secret away already. You must ask him," she told the king.

"She speaks of the young man whom you put to death because he would not fight the dragon," the courtier told the king. "He had the secret and now we shall never have it."

The king had never forgotten the young peasant. Drawing his sword, he faced the courtier. "You are wrong. The peasant gave us his secret, though we did not see it. He gave us the secret of living in his dying," said the king, dropping his sword to the ground, as he slowly walked away.

Lent, the forty days before Easter, is the symbolic way Christians leave behind the daily clamor of chores and confusions to say, "Yes" to God's call, to seek silence and solitude, peace and prayer, in order to hear God's whispers of love, his challenges of service, a time to give up those things that get in the way of our loving God and others.

PROGRAM ACTIVITIES:

1. Draw a symbol of your faith. What does the cross mean to you?

2. What was the "secret" in the story, "Secret In His Dying"? What was the symbolism of the "dragon"? Why was the dragon never found? What is your feeling, belief, about fighting? killing? What was the symbolism of the "lady of wisdom"?

3. Was the young man wise or foolish to die? Was Jesus wise or foolish to die? In fairy tales the oldest are clever and strong and the young are symbolic of the kind, gentle, blessed, holy, innocent, simpleton and fool. There are usually three and though the first two fail, the last, the simpleton, succeeds, is unassuming, receiving gifts for the journey that will aid him in his quest which the older do not want or think they need. Jesus is sometimes seen as the youngest, strong with the power of humility, doing what he must do, God's fool. Though he does not know how God's mission will be accomplished, he has confidence in the One who sends him.

"God does not see as people see," the foolish does not conform to the values of the world but to the values of God's kingdom. Discuss these values. How do they relate to you?

[1] Carroll, James, **Wonder and Worship**, Paulist Press, 1970.

YOUTH LOVE TO MIME

by Vivian Rosquist

When I think of the perfect youth activity, I think of something that will interest differing young people, foster increased scriptural understanding or growing faith, and allow maximum flexibility for busy leaders. For the Lenten season, I know of no better device than a narrative mime project. It is a project that can be as simple or elaborate as your circumstances and group allow and one that can be repeated from one year to the next. Best of all however, the passion and resurrection stories provide perfect narrative material and spiritual rewards for both youth and adults.

Probably the only prerequisite for doing a narrative mime based on scripture is for both the leaders and the youth to understand exactly what they are trying to do. For many people the mention of mime suggests only the most exaggerated forms of the art such as the very stylized technique called mannequin mime with its stiff, doll-like movement or else the exact, slow-motion movement that entertainers like Marcel Marceau use. In fact, mime includes any portrayal of stories or vignettes which are presented without any speaking. The kind of narrative mime which is suggested here involves a combination of devices including dramatic reading, creative movement, mime techniques, music, and lighting for visual effect. Your group can use its own ideas to make a totally unique mix of ingredients, but its primary goal should be the same as that of every scripture-based mime—to portray the word of God in spirit and truth so that it speaks to the hearts of viewers and enriches their experience of the gospel. As long as you keep this primary goal in mind and work together in a prayerful attitude, the project is sure to have a powerful effect on both the mime participants and the viewers.

Once your group understands this purpose and attitude, you can begin the project by having everyone read the gospel verses they would like to portray. Perhaps they will take turns reading aloud so that a narrator can be chosen. It will be important to have a person who can read the passages with energy and expressiveness to assume this position.

After the text is chosen, it must be read again so that a list of characters can be made. Don't worry if this list is longer than the number of young people in your group. One person will be able to play more than one part if necessary.

The next step is to find the sub-stories within the text. If you choose the passage beginning with Matthew 26:14, for example, you will find 13 sub-stories to portray beginning with Judas and the chief priests dealing for Jesus's betrayal and ending with Jesus's appearance to the two Marys after his resurrection.

Once you have the list of characters and have marked the specific verses for each sub-story, you'll be able to make a chart showing which characters appear in which scenes. Some characters like Peter and Jesus will appear often. The individuals who play these will take only one part. Other characters appear less frequently so that some players can take double parts as needed.

59

When all the parts have been assigned, the actual preparation of the mime begins with the process of blocking. If you intend to present your mime for an audience upon completion, it is important to do the blocking where the presentation will occur. Verse by verse, the narrator will read the chosen scripture and the players will experiment with a variety of postures and movements, trying to interpret the words with appropriate expressions and gestures. Those young people who aren't included in the verse being blocked will suggest movements and give critical comment to the players. Thus the whole group should be involved with creating the mime. Encourage the young people to imagine themselves really there in Bible times so that they can discuss the attitudes of the characters and the moods of the scenes as they work out physical movement to portray these things. Also remind them that movements include the whole body, not just head and arms. Kneeling, crouching, sitting, and prone positions are just as valid as standing ones. The face, however, should always be turned to the audience, at least in part.

Whenever the consensus of opinion forms that the movements are right for given verses because they accurately reflect the words of scripture, then the patterns of movement should be finalized. If the total passage isn't too long, you may choose to practice this verse several times as soon as it is blocked so that the movements are committed to memory as you go. If the passage you choose is quite long and complex, however, you may find it necessary to recruit an assistant director who will write down or diagram the movements of each scene. These notations can be very simple and brief, just enough to remind individuals of the planned moves. Once one verse is finalized, then the process continues with other verses and scenes.

One of the real advantges of this project is the great amount of flexibility it affords. If you and your group choose to spend several hours per week and work from Ash Wednesday until Easter on the project, you may be able to do the entire passage from Matthew including all 13 sub-stories. If the group has less time, they can begin the story with Jesus at the time of his arrest and finish at the sealed tomb. This version will have only 8 sub-stories and would be perfect for a Maundy Thursday or Good Friday presentation because it leaves viewers waiting for Easter Sunday and the resurrection. An even shorter version could begin with Pilate washing his hands and end with the appearance of angels to the two Marys at the empty tomb.

In all cases, part of the beauty of the narrative mime will be its simplicity. There will be no elaborate scenery to worry about and little costuming. If you have musical members in your group, they may enjoy enhancing your production with songs from Jesus Christ Superstar which echo the parts of scripture that are included in your narrative. If not, taped music would work equally well. Or maybe you'll have just one individual play instrumental interludes on guitar or flute at the points where one scene finishes and another begins. This technique will serve to highlight individual incidents because the mime actors will freeze in position during the music. It will also offer meditative pauses to the viewers and facilitate transitions for the players. The main thing is to use the imagination and talent of your particular young people to the best advantage. Don't forget to secure permission if you perform copyrighted material. And remember, too, that your mime can be a powerful worship experience without music - the music is merely an enhancing device.

Costume is another enhancing device. Even if your costumes are as simple as jeans and T-shirts, they can help identify characters so that the viewers follow the narrative more easily. The colors of the T-shirts, for example, can help portray something about each character. The chief priests might wear bold, bright colors to express wealth and high status. Judas, the betrayer, might wear red to set him apart

from the other disciples. The disciples and Jesus might wear browns and greys to show their position as ordinary people. After the resurrection, Jesus might appear in white.

For more elaborate costumes, you may choose to use a caftan pattern to make robes for each character in appropriate fabric. Or girls can wear leotards and tights while boys wear black slacks and turtleneck shirts. Again, the choices are wide open. You can be as simple or complicated as your situation suggests. One more enhancing device is lighting. Candles can provide illumination and create interesting shadows. A dimmer switch can help create mood. A clamp light can be used to cast harsh light on a scene of conflict or to spotlight a small side vignette. Again, the mime can be effective without extra light so keep it simple if that suits best.

The one device that can't be neglected is make-up. Mime make-up is very simple. It includes a white face which is made with either zinc oxide or clown white make-up. This extends in a circular shape from mid-forehead, around the face and along the jawline to the chin. This circle shape is outlined in black with an eyebrow pencil. Liquid eyeliner is then used to add three eye lines to each eye. One horizontal line starts at the outside corner of each eye and extends outward and two vertical lines begin above and below the center of each eye and extend upward and downward. The final touches include three red dots, one on each cheek and one on the tip of the nose, and a heart shape drawn at the center of the mouth. These marks can be made with cream rouge or lipstick.

Whatever else you choose to do, don't neglect the make-up. Especially for teens, who are prone to self-consciousness, the make-up is helpful in forgetting the self and entering into the character. It also helps the viewers focus on the scripture instead of seeing the familiar face playing a part.

When the mime has been blocked and rehearsed, the project becomes a ministry to others through presentation. Before presenting the mime, youth should be encouraged to understand spiritual mime not as a story they are acting for an audience, but as an expression of faith that can be shared with other believers. Pray with them, inviting the Holy Spirit to enter into your group and minister through your portrayal to the believers who view it. Both mime players and viewers will experience the scripture at a deeper spiritual level and the Lenten experience will be richer for everyone.

FIVE WORDS OF LENT
A CLOSE LOOK

by Judith Frenz

During the Lenten Season youth and their leaders can take a close look at five aspects of Lent.

Lent is Imposition. Have a group member look up the meaning of the word imposition and relate it to the rest of the group. On Ash Wednesday some churches reinact an ancient rite in which the foreheads of participants are marked with the sign of the cross using ashes from last year's palm leaves. This rite is called the "Imposition of Ashes". Remembering the meaning of the word imposition, this rite tells us something about Lent. Read Matthew 26:66-75 while the group follows along. Discuss how might Peter have felt when he realized he had "blown it"? How do we feel when we are reminded of the fact that we "blow it" (sin)? Are we able to do God's will all the time? Lent is an imposition because we do not like to be reminded that we need God's help and forgiveness.

Lent is a time of Evaluation. Lent is an Anglo-Saxon word meaning "long" and relating to the lengthening of day in Spring when nature struggles for rebirth. Read I Peter 2:9-10. Then share answers to these questions. What does the fact that we belong to God mean in our lives? What does it mean to repent? (Stress change - turning around - involved. There is more to it than just "feeling sorry".) What would you like to be doing five years from now? How much time do you spend watching TV? Studying? Helping others? Having fun? (Help them see the need for goals and balance.) During Lent we need to examine and evaluate where we are going and what we think is important.

Lent is Service. In John 13:4-5, 12-15, and John 13:34 we read of an action and a command of Jesus. What should the action and words mean to us, his followers? Should we help only people who "deserve it". Should we expect a reward? Lent is a season when we are reminded of Jesus' unselfish act of love for undeserving humankind. It is a time when we are urged to show unselfish love for others in service.

A fourth word to look at is Testing. Read Matthew 5:10-11 and discuss it. Is it easy to be a Christian? If someone asked you why you go to church and Sunday church school what would you tell them? Even if no one else in your family went would you still go?

Another aspect of Lent is Awareness. Read Mark 8:31-32 and then ask, "Can there be the joy of resurrection and new life of Easter without the sorrow and death of Lent? Lent is awareness- the truth is that Jesus must suffer and die for God's plan of salvation to be completed.

THE EASTER QUESTIONS

by Jean Rasmussen

CHARACTERS

Rodney Tyler

Geoffrey Lane   Mrs. Ella Horton

Patti Allen   Johnny Moran

Lynn Walker   Mark Boyle

NARRATOR:
"As you know, the Passover is two days away - and the Son of Man will be handed over to be crucified." NIV   (Matthew 26:2)

When the Lord Jesus said that, it raised questions in the minds of the disciples. There are questions in the minds of people today regarding his death, burial and resurrection. In our Lenten playlet, we will see how some of our college students handle them.

ACT I - Office of the college paper.
(Rodney, Geoffrey and Patti are seated at a long table working on plans for the next edition of **Campus Comments.** *Clippings, notepads, a Bible and textbooks are spread on the table.)*

RODNEY:
(Looks through clippings.) Here's an article on Lent. *(Speaks as though addressing another person.)* Excuse me, sir, I wonder if you would mind telling the readers of **Campus Comments** just what your feeling are at this Lenten season?

PATTI:
(Tapping pencil.) Not bad. In fact, I'd say that's pretty good. I wonder what people are thinking?

GEOFFREY:
(Frowning.) I think it's too vague. We need something with more of a punch. A lot of people don't even think about Lent.

63

PATTI:

I suppose you're right, but I like the idea of making the question something related to Easter.

RODNEY:

(Puts the clipping down.) I'm open to suggestion. We've been here three quarters of an hour and have covered everything but the questions for the inquiring photographer. Since I'm that person, I'd sure like to have some help with questions.

PATTI:

I wish Lynn had come to the meeting. She usually has some good ideas.

GEOFFREY:

(More amiably.) She'll be here tomorrow and there's no reason why we have to make a decision today.

RODNEY:

(Turning to Geoffrey.) You're right. We've had some good discussion and have the layout in rough form. Now, maybe we should think it over until our meeting tomorrow.

PATTI:

(Smiling.) I agree, but shouldn't we decide just one or two things we want to center our questions around?

RODNEY:

Just what do you mean?

PATTI:

For instance, will we be asking more than one question? Will it be about the holidays?

RODNEY:

Let's say the core has to have something to do with the holidays and something more personal. That's two major questions.

PATTI:

Good. And I'll be sure to call Lynn so she can be working toward the same goals. I'll have to leave now. *(Glances at watch.)* I'm going to the Campus Prayer Group, anyone want to come? *(Picks up her books and Bible.)*

RODNEY:

Not me.

GEOFFREY:

(Rises.) Me either. See you tomorrow. *(Picks up his books and leaves with Patti and Rodney following him.)*

LIGHTS DIMMED

ACT II - Office of the college paper.

(Rodney, Geoffrey and Lynn are seated at the table waiting for Patti.)

RODNEY:

I hope you've done some thinking, because when we walk out of here, I'm going to need at least two questions I can ask the people on the street. And my suggestions weren't very good.

LYNN:

I'm counting on Patti.

GEOFFREY:

(Begins writing on notepaper.) Just give me a few more minutes and I'll have my questions ready.

RODNEY:

Patti mentioned Easter. Any more thoughts about that?

LYNN:

We did talk about it and she seems to have a pretty good one. It's... *(Patti enters and Lynn turns to her.)* We were just talking about you, but I'll let you tell them your idea.

RODNEY:

Yes, let's hear it. At least it may spark something that is workable.

PATTI:

I think first I'd like to hear your ideas. I did most of the talking last time.

RODNEY:

Our suggestions are a little scarce.

GEOFFREY:

(Stops writing.) I have one. How about asking what the students would think of a trip to Florida next year for Easter? For a second question, you could ask which beach they would prefer to stay at.

RODNEY:

There's just one problem with that. Interviewing people on the street is our only community outreach.

LYNN:

Every other time, though, we've tied it in with campus activities, like the time we asked: "Can you tell us what your opinion is of the plans for a new gymnasium?" Remember that one?

PATTI:

Yes, but this is the first interview which has come during Lent and I still think we should tie it in with the holiday.

GEOFFREY

It doesn't really matter to me. So let's hear your idea, Patti.

RODNEY:

Yes, let's hear it.

PATTI:

(Takes out a sheet of paper.) The two questions are: Do you think we should have the same date each year for Easter, and what does Easter mean to you?

RODNEY:

(Looks puzzles.) I hate to be so dumb, but why do we have a different date each year for Easter?

PATTI:

It has something to do with the full moon and the sun, I think. Geoffrey, you're our science major. What is the reason?

GEOFFREY:

Yes, it's determined by the sun and moon. Easter comes the first Sunday after the full moon following the vernal equinox.

LYNN:

(Scratches her head.) The vernal what?

GEOFFREY:

That's the time when the sun crosses the plane of the earth's equator and makes day and night of equal length.

RODNEY:

(Addressing Geoffrey.) Very good explanation, but what about the questions Patti suggested? What do you think of them?

GEOFFREY:

They're not bad. At least they're not too religious. *(Looks at Patti teasingly and smiles.)*

RODNEY:

I have no objection to asking those questions. What do you think, Lynn?

LYNN:

I think the idea is great just so long as you use people of different ages so you get a cross-section.

PATTI:

Right. *(Smiles at Geoffrey.)* And while the questions aren't too religious, I think what we believe about Easter is very important because it is the resurrection of God's Son who died for our sins.

LIGHTS DIMMED

ACT III - Street corner

(Rodney is standing on a street corner. A bus stop sign is at the other end. He is adjusting his camera. A housewife with a full shopping bag walks toward the bus stop.)

RODNEY:

Excuse me. I'm the inquiring photograper from **Campus Comments.** Would you let me have your picture and the answers to a few questions? *(Takes out a pad and pencil.)*

MRS. HORTON:

Yes, I'd be glad to.

RODNEY:

First, what is your name? And what do you do for a living?

MRS. HORTON:

I'm Mrs. Ella Horton and I work at the Village Bakery.

RODNEY:

(Raises his camera.) All right, Mrs. Horton, if you will smile, I'll take your picture. *(Snaps picture.)* There. Now, tell me what you think about having the same date each year for Easter? And what does Easter mean to you?

MRS. HORTON:

The same date? Yes, I think it would be a good idea. It would help us with our ordering at the bakery. And it would help me with my own plans, too.

RODNEY:

At home or in your church?

MRS. HORTON:

Oh, at home. I don't have time for church. I work longer hours around the holidays. *(Taking white bag from shopping bag and hands it to him.)* Here, would you like one of our cookies?

RODNEY:

(Selects one and takes a bite.) Delicious, really delicious. I'll have to stop by your bakery sometime. Thank you.

MRS. HORTON:

(Smiles with satisfaction.) We do have some good pastry and that's my Easter. *(Exits.)*

(A high school student approaches Rodney from the opposite direction. He is counting dollars and putting them in his wallet.)

RODNEY:

(Completes his notes about Mrs. Horton.) Say, you look like you just got paid. I'm from **Campus Comments**. Mind if I take your picture and ask you a few questions?

JOHNNY:

(Straightens up and smiles.) Sure. Why not?

RODNEY:

(Snaps picture.) What is your name and what do you do to earn that much money? *(Gets ready to jot down notes.)*

JOHNNY:

My name's Johnny Moran and that isn't my money. It belongs to my uncle. I've been selling balloons for him.

RODNEY:

Sure looks like you've sold a lot of them.

JOHNNY:

Yeah, I have.

RODNEY:

Now, let me ask you a couple of questions. What do you think about having the same date each year for Easter?

JOHNNY:
Doesn't much matter to me.

RODNEY:
What does Easter mean to you?

JOHNNY:
(Pointing to himself.) To me? Balloons and more balloons. My uncle sells almost as many balloons at Easter as he sells on the Fourth of July. Soon we'll be over in the park for the Easter egg hunt and today I've been downtown where everyone is shopping.

RODNEY:
Well, have yourself a good time and thanks for the answers.

JOHNNY:
I've got to hurry. See ya. *(Exits.)*

RODNEY:
So long. *(Rodney jots down notes as a fellow carrying a tennis racket approaches him from the direction in which Johnny came.)*

RODNEY:
(Smiles and nods.) Hi, there. Mind if I take your picture and ask a couple of questions for our **Campus Comments**?

MARK:
Go right ahead.

RODNEY:
First, your name.

MARK:
I'm Mark Boyle, the youth pastor at the campus church.

RODNEY:
(They shake hands.) I'm pleased to meet you. I'm Rodney Tyler, a business major at the college. Now, for a good pose. *(Takes picture and jots down name.)* All right, tell me, do you think we should have the same date each year for Easter?

MARK:
Well, I don't think it affects the real meaning of Easter. But, yes, I guess I'd be in favor of it.

RODNEY:
You're a good one to answer this second question: What does Easter mean to you?

MARK:
Because it's the resurrection of the Lord Jesus, it means everything. Without the empty tomb, we couldn't have eternal life in heaven. *(Rodney jots down the answer.)* Don't you agree?

RODNEY:
Well, I guess I've never thought about it too much. Oh, I went to church school when I was young... *(Pauses.)*

MARK:

Did you ever accept Christ as your Savior?

RODNEY:

I believe in him ... and sometimes I pray.

MARK:

The Bible does say, "Believe on the Lord Jesus Christ and thou shalt be saved." It means with the heart, though, not just with the mind. The next thing to do is to commit your life to him. As the Bible says, "To me to live is Christ."

RODNEY:

There's a girl who works with us on **Campus Comments** who belongs to your church. Her name is Patti Allen.

MARK:

Oh, yes, I know the Allens. Her younger brother is one of the fellows I'm going to meet at the tennis courts. It's a part of our youth activity for this week.

RODNEY:

I'd better not hold you up then.

MARK:

Look, we'd like to have you come to our dawn service. We have a breakfast after it for campus students. It's at 6:00 A.M. Easter morning over in the park where they give the concerts. Try to make it if you can.

RODNEY:

Thanks a lot. I've never been to one and maybe I will try to be there. *(Jots notes in his pad.)* Well, I guess that wraps it up for today. Cookies, balloons and an Easter dawn service. Maybe I will get God into the picture this year, and make Him Lord of my life. I guess that's why Patti is different. She believes with her whole heart that Jesus died for her.

MARK:

Do that and we will be looking for you. *(Waves and exits.)*

NARRATOR:

What does Easter mean to you? A vacation, fun and candy, or is it time when you celebrate Jesus' death and resurrection for you. Jesus said, "I am the resurrection and the life. He who believes in me will live, even though he dies; and whoever lives and believes in me will never die. Do you believe this?" NIV (John 11:25)

This Easter be sure Jesus is Lord of your life.

LUMEN CHRISTI:
THE LIGHT OF CHRIST

by Colleen Britton

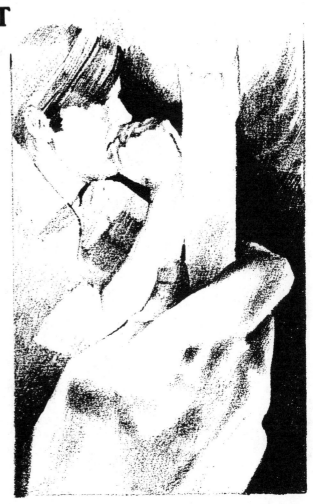

For centuries candles have been used in churches and in homes to symbolize and remind us of Christ, the light of the world. During Advent (prior to Christmas) four candles representing hope, love, peace, and joy surround the taller central "Christ Candle" which is lit on Christmas Eve to celebrate his birth. Every year at Easter time in the Greek Orthodox Church there is a special service called "Phos" meaning "The Light". The sanctuary is darkened except for the Christ candle. The eldest son or male member of each family lights a candle from the Christ candle and carefully carries the "Light of Christ" home to light all the candles and lamps in the home for the new year.

This tradition can be modified as the "Light of Christ" is brought into every home in the congregation. Use the large Christ candle that was lit on Christmas and carve a cross in it as a reminder of Easter. At the Sunday worship service just prior to Lent, or at a special Ash Wednesday service the candle can again be lit and its symbolism explained. The candle can then be passed from family to family each day of Lent. If your congregation is large, several candles can be used. Passing the candle from family to family not only provides an opportunity to learn more about Christ, but it helps people within the congregation to get better acquainted with one another.

A study/discussion or worship guide can be sent along with the candle to help families deepen their understanding of what "Christ, the light of the world" means. Suggested Scripture reading may include: Psalm 27:1, Psalm 119:105, Isaiah 60:19, Matthew 5:14-16, and John 8:12.

70

GIVING MEANING

TO LENT

by Elaine M. Ward

Lent is a journey toward change, toward a renewal of heart.

God said,"I will remove from them their heart of stone and give them a heart of flesh." (Ezekiel 11:19b)

Lent is the time of choice...to choose a heart of stone or a heart of flesh. Lent is a time of dedicated thought, prayer, and study concerning choosing, changing, and renewal.

1. In silence think about the most difficult choice you are now facing. Write it in one sentence. Are there ways God can help you with this choice through people, prayer, or scripture?

2. Choose a partner and share an experience of an encounter with a person whose heart was "of stone." As you think about this encounter, was there any way it could have been or now could be changed "to flesh?" Have you ever felt your heart as hard as stone? Name a story, book, or movie in which you witnessed a person whose heart was "of flesh."

3. Read or tell the story, "The Banjo Man."[1] If you do not have this book, here is a synopsis of the story.

David, a young jogger, hurts his foot while jogging and sits on a log pondering the question, "What shall I do with my life?" He is approached by a stranger who soothes his sore foot by rubbing it, and then he rubs the other one as well. David is filled immediately with a sense of rhythm of dance.

From that moment David begins to dance. Dancing along the road to the city he encounters an army recruiter, and David offers him his service. When David is told that his feet are not for dancing but for marching, he dances on down the road to a monastery.

There he tells the abbot that he has been praying since sunrise just by dancing and is at peace with God, with the world and everything, and he wants to devote his entire life to the church. The abbot is shocked and David again dances away, this time offering his services to the business world.

David is offended by the thought of using his dancing for selling "people what they don't need and pretending that it will make them dance or be happy."

In place after place David meets the same negative response, and broke, out of work, and alone, he enters a church to rest and observes a large crucifix.

Suddenly the Christ figure from the crucifix kneels to soothe his feet and then to dance with David, until the priest and the police interrupt, but not before David knows "the truth and I shall never stop dancing in good times or in bad."

71

As he sat on the old fallen tree and rubbed his foot, his mind was filled with a rush of thoughts. This morning his thoughts seemed clearer than ever before. They were not new thoughts, only clearer than before: "What shall I do with my life? What will be my life's work? It was so much simpler in the ancient days. The choices were easier: knight, clergyman, merchant, or peasant. A son did the work of his father. But today so many choices confront one; which choice is the right one?

4. Discuss: What shall I do with my life? What shall be my life's work? What choices are available to you? How do you decide "Which choice is the right one?" What do you enjoy doing? Whom do you enjoy serving? What is your favorite subject at school? Would you be interested in persons sharing their careers with the group?

5. Take off your shoes and socks and rub each other's feet. If you prefer, rub your own feet instead. Massage the muscles of the bottom of the foot and then the ankle and the toes, one by one. How does it feel?

The stranger who massaged David's feet said, "Our feet are very important. All the organs and muscles in our body have nerve endings in our feet. Hundreds of thousands of tiny nerves all gather there from different parts of the body."

6. Dance the Lord's Prayer. When David danced to the monastery, he told the abbot, "I've been praying ever since sunrise just by dancing."

"You are called dancer...one who catches the rhythms of life and love and gives them form."[2]

See "Worship via Choreography," **CHURCH EDUCATOR**, January 1979, for suggested choreography for dancing the Lord's Prayer and a bibliography of books on creative movement at the end of the article.
(Available from Educational Ministries, Inc)

7. Read Romans 10:15 aloud, "How beautiful are the feet of those who bring good news!" Discuss: What are the rhythms of your life at this time? How can you give them form? How can you invite others to join you in the dance so that together you may praise and exalt the God who gives you life and other gifts? Do you believe that persons can pray by dancing?

8. Have a debate. As David danced along the road, David thought his question, "What shall I do with my life?", had been answered, but not as he expected. He thought: "It really didn't seem important what you do in life; it's how you do it. If you do it with harmony and in harmony, all is beautiful and all is prayerful."

Ask the participants to choose whether they agree or disagree with the above. Those who agree go to one side of the room and discuss their reasons and prepare for a panel discussion or debate. Those who disagree, to the other side of the room and also prepare. Ask each group to choose two persons to be on the panel. Discuss the issue for fifteen minutes. Then open the discussion to the entire group.

Recall that Lent is a period of choice and change. They are free to change their opinions as they listen and talk. Encourage them to give illustrations from their own experiences that support their argument.

9. Discuss the symbolism of David's "dancing." As David is taken away by the police, he says, "Now I know the truth, and I shall never stop dancing again, in good times or in bad." What other symbol or word could be substituted for "dancing" as the "truth" in your life? Why was the hero of the story named David?

10. Share poetry. Lent is renewing the heart, the heart of flesh. It is entering the solitude and communion of God's will and way. In peace and prayer, listen to these words of the last week in the life of Jesus. Ask for volunteers to read each one of the following poems[3] in sequence, allowing silence and a time for meditation between each reading.

ANOINTING AT BETHANY
Matthew 26:6-13

The woman in the house of Simon poured costly oil or perfume over Jesus' head and Jesus' friends criticized her. But

72

Jesus said they would always have the poor with them.

> With a smile she flung good sense away
> And would be remembered from that day
> As the one who loved our Lord so much,
> She spent her last cent on oil, or such,
> To pour upon his head to signify
> Jesus' anointing. He must die
> To set us free
> To love, as the woman whom he,
> Jesus, told his friends had done so well
> To spend her all upon the Father's Son!

THE LAST SUPPER
Matthew 26:20-29

The Passover Feast was eaten on Maundy Thursday. Jesus ate The Last Supper in Jerusalem with his disciples as a farewell and promise that God's community would continue.

> It's the Lord's supper, please come in.
> Everyone's ready, time to begin.
> "This is my body," Jesus said,
> "Given for you," as he broke the bread.
> "This is the blood of the covenant, drink it up,"
> Jesus said, as he took the cup.
> "This is my promise, this is my vow,
> I'll be with you always, as I'm with you now.
> This is my promise, this is my plea,
> Drink of my cup and eat with me
> Now and forever through eternity."

JESUS IN GETHSEMANE
Matthew 26:36-46

It was against the law to leave Jerusalem on Maundy Thursday, so Jesus could not return to Bethany after the supper with his disciples. Jesus went to the garden just outside the walls of Jerusalem to pray, to struggle with his feelings about death. Would he die before his work was done or was this part of his Father's will?

Jesus enemies came with weapons. Although Jesus could have been arrested any time, they came at night, for it is in the dark that we hope to hide evil deeds. At this time the disciples ran away.

> Oh, that I could say "No" like a child
> And rest or run away and hide
> In the wilderness before I died.
> But You, O Lord, are at my side.
> Now be my guide and give me strength
> To do Your will and take my hand

> So I will stay to face and fight and die
> And live again, as You, O Lord, have planned.

JUDAS' BARGAIN
Matthew 26:14-16

The chief priests and scribes were seeking how they could arrest Jesus by stealth and kill him. They did not want to do it during the feast for fear they would stir up the crowds. Jesus is aware of this and tells his friends so, to which they reply, "Is it I?"

Judas, the betrayer, had given Jesus' enemies a sign, saying, "The one I shall kiss is the man; seize him and lead him away safely."

> Judas, Judas, what is this,
> Betraying Jesus with a kiss?
> Judas, Judas, don't you know
> This is God's son, he showed you so!
> Judas, why did you betray
> The one who taught you how to pray?
>
> Judas, Judas, you're like me!
> Forgive me, Lord, for when I flee
> Good and right and all that's true,
> And like Judas betray you, too.

PETER'S DENIAL
Mark 14:66-72

In the courtyard, while Peter was waiting to see what would happen to his Lord, a maiden recognized him and told him so. Peter denied that he knew Jesus nor understood what she meant. The second time a maiden said, "This man is one of them," Peter again denied it. The third person is certain that Peter is one of them and Peter swears, "I do not know this man of whom you speak." At that moment the cock crows a second time, and Peter breaks down and weeps.

> "You were with him. I'm sure that you must be
> A friend of his." "I know him not!" said he.
> "This man is one of them," again he heard,
> And swore, "I do not know this man.
> I swear my word!"
> The cock crowed twice!
> And while the maiden swept,
> Peter heard his Lord's last words and wept.

THE COURT TRIAL
AND CRUCIFIXION
Mark 14 and 15

Jesus' trial was at night before Caiaphas, but the high priest could find no way to trap Jesus. He sent him to Pilate, who could give the death penalty. Pilate was a weak man and let the crowd decide who should be set free. Then Pilate washed his hands of any resposibility in the matter.

Jesus carried his cross to the place of the skull, Golgatha, to die by crucifixion, a death by torture, nailed to the cross and left there to die from thirst, exposure, and lack of circulation in his body. It was the custom to give the condemned wine with a drug in it to lessen the pain, but Jesus refused. It was also the custom to hang a sign around the guilty one telling the reason for his death. Around Jesus' neck they put the sign saying,"Jesus of Nazareth, King of the Jews."

They nailed him to a cross on Golgotha,
"Place of the skull,"
And left him there to die,
Remembering the paid and angry crowd
In Pilate's court and their cry,
"Crucify!"
Between two thieves he hung,
"King of the Jews"
On that Good Friday
When the day turned night
Inside a topsy-turvy world where God had
Once again, in love, made all things right!

EASTER
Mark 16:1-20

God kept His promise and Jesus kept his and on Easter Sunday was resurrected from the dead.

They saw him on the cross,
They heard him cry,
"Father, it is over!"
They saw him die.
They saw them take him down
And bury him.
They saw him live again
And talk with them.
They saw...they heard...they knew
What had been done.
That Christ had risen from the dead
And God had won!

[1] Edward Hays, *Twelve and One Half Keys*, Forest of Peace Books, Route One, Box 247, Easton, KS 66020, 1981.

[2] *Lenten Devotional*, Fifth National Clown, Mime, Dance, and Puppetry Ministry Workshop, Chicago, August, 1982.

[3] Elaine M. Ward, *New Testament Stories*, Educational Ministries, Inc., Walnut, CA., 1984.

WHO AM I?

by Vivan Rosquist

Many people played a part in the events leading up to and immediately following the crucifixion of Jesus. See how many you can recognize by matching the statements on the left with the people who could have made them on the right. CLUE: Some statements can be matched with more than one name and one person's name can also be the correct answer for more than one statement.

1. I denied Jesus three times just as He said I would.

2. I washed my hands to show that the responsibility for Jesus' death was not mine.

3. I helped Jesus carry his cross.

4. They brought Jesus to my house to be questioned after he was arrested.

5. I betrayed Jesus for 30 pieces of silver.

6. At the crucifixion, Jesus promised me that I would be in paradise with him.

7. I fell asleep while waiting for Jesus in the Garden of Gethsemane.

8. I could not believe Jesus was alive until I put my finger on the nail scars of his hands and my hand to his side.

9. I was released from prison when the crowd chose to crucify Jesus and let me go free.

10. I was the first person to see Jesus after the resurrection.

11. I used my sword to cut off the right ear of Malchus, the High Priest's servant, when he came with the Roman soldiers to arrest Jesus.

12. I went to Pilate for permission to take Jesus' body. Then I wrapped the body in clean linen and placed it in my own tomb.

13. I was in the empty tomb when the women came with spices to embalm Jesus' body. I told them to go tell the disciples that Jesus had been raised and was going ahead of them to Galilee.

Caiaphas

James

Barabbas

a criminal

John

an angel

Peter

Joseph of Arimathea

Pilate

Simon of Cyrene

Thomas

Judas

Mary Magdalene

Answers and texts:

1. Peter (Luke 23:54-60)
2. Pilate (Matthew 27:24)
3. Simon of Cyrene (Luke 23:26)
4. Caiaphas (Matthew 26:57)
5. Judas (Matthew 26:14,15)
6. a criminal (Luke 23:39-43)
7. Peter, James, John (Mark 14:32,33)
8. Thomas (John 20:24-28)
9. Barabbas (Mark 15:15)
10. Mary Magdalene (Mark 16:9)
11. Peter (John 18:10)
12. Joseph of Arimathea (Matthew 27:57-60)
13. an angel (Mark 16:5-7)

Note to Leaders:

This activity can be done individually as a self-quiz or the group can be divided into teams who will race to see who can complete the activity correctly. For older youth you may want to change the format from matching to fill-in-the blank and give the gospel texts as hints.

JESUS IS RISEN:
WHAT ARE YOU SAYING?

by Robert G. Davidson

This is a four-part KNOWING YOUR FAITH series for senior high young people. The basic theme of this series will be on Jesus and the meaning of the resurrection. This material might be used as a senior high youth ministry program, or as a special study program on Sunday mornings of weekday afternoons. It might also be adapted to use with college and young adult groups, or in a church school teaching/learning program series.

SESSION I

Only the person who understands his or her faith can make it understandable to another person, and have an answer when he or she is asked what faith is. What we hope is that through a series of programs such as this one that persons might be led toward a meaningful understanding of their faith insofar as faith can ever be understandable. We are always in a process of change through growth, new life experiences, opportunities, struggles, hurts, and joys, causing our understanding of faith to change.

The resurrection of Jesus is the very cornerstone of the Christian Church. "If Jesus had not been raised, then the message of the Church is in vain" (I Corinthians 15:14). The resurrection is the best known belief about Jesus. The importance of the resurrection for Christians cannot be overstated. It is the climax of the story of Jesus and the only adequate reason for the growth and spread of Christianity. It is the one explanation for the amazing change from fear and defeat into courage and meaningful hope in the lives of the early Christians. It alone can explain their church, their Sunday, their New Testament and their confidence in life after death. The fact that God raised Jesus from the dead became the unanimous and most assured reason for faith of his disciples and early followers. How Jesus was raised they never explained nor did they give identical testimonies about their experiences. A unique, unparallel event, it is the greatest miracle in the story of Jesus and the most positive evidence of the power and the purpose of God.

Therefore, conversation about the resurrection of Jesus means talking about the faith of the Church. If Jesus' resurrection is a matter of uncertainty, faith itself will be a matter of uncertainty also.

The basic statement for our study is: **JESUS IS RISEN.** Concerning this statement there is complete agreement. There is no Christian who would not be able to give his or her agreement to the importance and centrality of this statement. Nor is there any Christian theologian who would not agree with it. This fact alone would suggest this sentence as a starting point for the study of the resurrection event.

But first we need to point out that there is a distinction between what we say and what we mean to say. So often we are easily inclined to read our ideas into words, and to think that ours is the only correct way in which the words can be used. It becomes important to accept the idea in exactly the same words. A distinction must be made between what we say and what we mean. When two persons say the same thing it does not follow that they mean the same thing. The basic statement JESUS IS RISEN, therefore, it seems, must be followed by the question: WHAT DOES THIS MEAN?

To begin the first program the leader might summarize the above material in his or her own words as an opening presentation for the group. Follow this by discussing the biblical passage I Corinthians 15:14, drawing as many comments and reactions to the statement from the group as possible. Each person's response, ideas, and concepts should be respected, and not questioned or evaluated. This first session should be used to stimulate thinking and interest in the topic.

Next, give a 3 x 5 card to each person and ask him/her to write a short statement defining what he/she feels the statement JESUS IS RISEN means to him/her. Collect the cards after everyone has finished the statements. (You may also want them to state what they believe their church leaders mean when they use the statement JESUS IS RISEN. Or, what does it mean in the Apostles' Creed or your own church's Statement of Faith.) Spend some time discussing the different ideas and concepts expressed. The following statements were made by a study group responding to this same statement. You may want to list some of these responses on a chalkboard for discussion also.

JESUS IS RISEN means:

—That the Christ consciousness is upper-most in my heart and mind.

—That we, too, have the promise of everlasting life.

—He conquered death in that he achieved immortality in the hearts on men.

—Jesus has passed from life on earth to whatever existence follows thereafter.

—Not much, because I am not sure I believe this but I still believe I am a Christian.

—Jesus is remembered and is the guide for my life.

—The beginning of a new world, a new age.

—Jesus was resurrected spiritually and is alive today as an example for me to follow.

—What Jesus taught still lives.

—His influence is spreading out over the world, no longer confined to a mortal body.

—Jesus is with us today.

Continue the conversation by discussing each of the three words in the statement. Write the three words across the top of a chalkboard JESUS IS RISEN. Under each word list what the group members believe the word says or means to them. Consider the word JESUS as an example: Does it mean the man Jesus of Nazareth? Or, does it mean Jesus as the Christ? Or, does it mean the Son of God? And, if so, what does that mean?

Then consider the word IS, which seems to be so simple. The stress might be placed on the present. As an illustration you might ask why they accept the good news of Jesus, who after all lived a long time ago and was crucified among an ancient people. A person might respond: "Jesus, I believe, is not a man belonging to the past but rather a living person. To me, Jesus lives and is of great concern to me today."

On the other hand the stress might be placed on the past. In this situation the statement becomes information about a past event and does not call for any personal involvement on the part of a Christian person today.

The most difficult problem is with defining the word RISEN. There are many responses that might be given. Your group will probably develop a long list of definitions under this word. Questions will develop like: Does Risen mean bodily risen? Of course, how does one define bodily? Does one interpret it in a spiritual sense? Or, are you thinking of Jesus as being in the hearts of his disciples? Or, has God acted in a way that we human beings do not begin to understand?

Conclude this program with a review of the basic key questions which have been developed to this point in the conversation. Point out that during future programs the study focus will be on the resurrection events as presented in the four Gospels and other early church traditions.

SESSION II

The four Gospels are parallel in thought and theme but are reports of the same event from four different witnesses. As one begins a study of the Gospels they should be aware of the so-called "two source theory", concerning Matthew, Mark and Luke. According to this theory, Mark's Gospel was the first to be written. Matthew and Luke knew Mark's writings and used it in their own writing, particularly to the extent of following its general plan. In addition, both had as a second source, that which is known as the "Q" source, a collection of sayings, largely the sayings of Jesus. Finally, Matthew and Luke used a certain amount of independent material. The two-source theory can therefore be represented as follows:

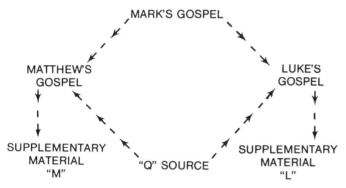

What is important for our study is that Matthew and Luke knew and used Mark's account of the Passion narrative and the Easter events when they compiled their own. But they expanded Mark's, using other traditions.

Throughout any study of the Gospels, one must remember that each Gospel depicts a unity, and must *not* be arbitrarily chopped up into pieces. We must never forget this, even when we are concentrating on the material presented in one particular section.

THE GOSPEL OF MARK — The earliest of the Gospels, Mark, has the shortest account of the resurrection. Mark points out that on the first day of the week, soon after sunrise, three woman, Mary Magdalene, Mary and Salome, came to the tomb to prepare the body of Jesus properly for burial. It was the custom to bury a body on the day of death but the Sabbath had prevented the care of the body. Since the stone was too great for the woman to roll aside, they wondered who would move it for them. The tomb was situated so that they looked up and saw it open. They entered and saw a young man in white robes. He had supernatural knowledge of their situation such as an angel might possess (a messenger of God). He calmed their amazement, told them they sought Jesus who had risen and showed them the empty place. The women were to go and tell the disciples and

Peter that Jesus was going to Galilee as he had promised (Mark 16:7). There they would see him. Astonished and trembling, they fled from the tomb and told no one through fear. Mark's Gospel ends abruptly with no report of the appearance to fulfill the forecasts given by Jesus to the disciples or the promise of the angel. There is no way to settle the question about the ending of Mark. It may be complete or incomplete. Since Mark knew of the resurrection, it is argued that his climax would contain an account of the appearance of Jesus. But Mark may have thought his previous promises of the resurrection were sufficient and that the right result of the tremendous truth of resurrection was an amazing reverence. His report establishes the fact of the empty tomb with the promise Jesus would be seen in Galilee.

There is an ending in Mark (16:9-20) which is canonical scripture though not written by Mark and is later than Matthew and Luke. It differs in thought and style from Mark. It contains no report of an appearance of Jesus at the empty tomb or in Galilee. The first appearance of Jesus was to Mary Magdalene alone who reported to those who had been with him that she had seen Jesus. The second appearance was to two individuals walking in the country. This is based on Luke's story of the walk to Emmaus. The third appearance was to the Eleven. This is similiar to Luke's report. In each of these appearances the followers of Jesus did not believe. The appendix to Mark is a short teaching which condemns unbelief, encourages belief and enumerates the resurrection appearances. Jesus not only rebuked the disciples for unbelief but he commanded them to preach the Gospel to the whole creation.

SUGGESTED PROCEDURE

1. During the first session the conversation centered around the phrase JESUS IS RISEN and the meaning each person found in the phrase. This session might begin with the leader briefly reviewing some of the concepts which were expressed during that first session.

2. The leader might present the above background material on the two-source theory on the development of the first three Gospels — Matthew, Mark and Luke. It might also be pointed out that John's Gospel was written about 30 years after Mark compiled his material — around AD 70. It is in any case highly improbable that the author of the Fourth Gospel knew any of

the other three Gospels, at least, he certainly did not make use of them.

3. Each person should have a Bible available — preferably several different versions of the Bible should be available for use by different persons. Have two or three persons read aloud from different versions, first Mark 15:40-47 — discuss briefly what is taking place in this passage. Second, have two or three persons read aloud Mark 16:1-8a, again briefly discussing what is happening. Follow this with the reading of Mark 16:8b-20 — pointing out that this is an appendix to Mark's Gospel and written by another author.

4. Ask everyone to close their Bibles and write a statement of their own on the events taking place in Mark 15:40 thru 16:8a. In other words, what would they write in a letter to a friend about these events. After everyone has had an opportunity to complete their statements, ask several persons to share theirs with the whole class. Questions might include: Did you find this difficult to write? Do you feel you had enough information available? Do you feel that you convinced the persons you were writing your letter to the true significance of this God-centered event which has taken place? After thinking about this would you now like to write your letter again, believing you could share this event in a more convincing way?

5. Spend some time now developing a group statement on what the author of Mark's Gospel was trying to communicate to his readers as he wrote those concluding passages to his Gospel. What were the feelings, the hopes, the dreams of this "Good News" communicator?

Finish by reviewing briefly the events of Jesus' ministry:

—his reaching out to all persons no matter who or what they were

—his reaching out to individual persons

—his teaching that the kingdom of God is within you

—his statement, "I will be with you always"

—his message that "God cares about you as an individual person"

—his dynamic impact and influence on all persons he came in contact with

—his joyful entry into the Holy City of Jerusalem on Palm Sunday with the crowds celebrating his coming

—his Last Supper with his disciples

—his arrest at Gethsemane

—his trial before Pilate and the crowds now calling for his death

—his disciples running away in fear for their lives and deserting him

—his crucifixion, his death!

—HIS RESURRECTION!

SESSION III

THE GOSPEL OF MATTHEW — Matthew combines two important thoughts in his resurrection material: the empty tomb and the appearances of Jesus both in Jerusalem and Galilee. Two women go at dawn to the tomb but there is no mention of their intent to prepare the body. A great earthquake takes place and an awesome angel rolls back the stone which is covering the entrance to the tomb, and the guards fall into a state of unconsciousness. The message to the women is the same as in Mark except that they are urged to go quickly to tell the disciples but there is no mention of Peter which is unusual in a Gospel which exalts him. The women run with fear and great joy to tell the disciples. On their way they encounter Jesus who greets them. Matthew then gives the report of the guards to the priests, who bribes them to say that the disciples stole the body as they slept and who promised to safeguard them from Pilate. The reference "to this day" shows a lapse of time and the spread of this rumor rather than probable fact.

Matthew completes his Gospel with the Great Commission. This second appearance of Jesus is at a mountain in Galilee where his disciples both worshiped and doubted him. The final words of Jesus are a summary of the Christian message. They establish the faith of the Christian church in its mission and its relationship to Jesus.

THE GOSPEL OF LUKE — Luke has carefully constructed his narratives of the resurrection event. He has a longer and more complete account, which includes the empty tomb, but places the appearances of Jesus in or near Jerusalem and not at the tomb, with no appearances in Galilee. About half of his narrative is given to the matchless Emmaus story. He is interested in showing the kind of body Jesus possessed and that he continued teaching and that he appeared to a number of people. There are women named at the tomb and others unnamed. They did not find the body or see Jesus. The two angels in bright, white clothing did tell of the resurrection of Jesus, although some translations do contain an announcement. The question of the angels, "Why do you look for the living among the dead?" assumes that Jesus had risen. Rather than stating that they would see Jesus in Galilee, the angels remind the women of the words of Jesus in Galilee about betrayal, crucifixion and resurrection. The women repeat these words to the Eleven and also the others, but their story seemed unbelievable.

The two men that Jesus appeared to on the way to Emmaus are not known outside of this story. Their failure to recognize Jesus when he came up to them was due to some unusual inability which is stated but not explained. Their concern over the death of Jesus and the confusing reports of the women give Jesus an opportunity to question them. Their report about Jesus claimed that he was a prophet, who was very popular among the people and was thought of as the long awaited Messiah to his disciples. The experience of the women at the tomb, was described as a vision of angels who reported that Jesus was alive and that his body was gone. The climax of this story takes place in the evening in a home around a dinner table when the two recognized Jesus as he took bread and blessed it and gave it to them. At this point Jesus vanishes and the two men return to Jerusalem and find the Eleven and the others who report that Jesus has risen and had appeared to Peter. There is no description of this second appearance.

The third appearance comes while they talked and Jesus suddenly is standing among them. He calms their fear of him as a possible ghost and quiets their troubled thoughts. Then he encourages them to feel his hands and feet and to know then that it is really him, and then he eats a piece of fish.

These reports by Luke omit any appearances of Jesus at the tomb. Appearances take place in or near Jerusalem. Other persons like the women and friends of the disciples share the appearances. This larger group of persons who share in the experience of the resurrection is in keeping with Luke's universal outreach of the Christian message. The stories of the appearances mingled disbelief and great joy as Luke stresses both evidence of the heart and mind — an inner recognition and evidence to the physical senses.

SUGGESTED PROCEDURE

1. Each person should have a Bible available — preferably several different versions of the Bible should be available for use by different persons. Have two or three people read out loud from different versions, first Matthew 28, then discuss briefly what is taking place in this passage. Second, have two or three read aloud Luke 24, again briefly discussing what is happening.

2. List on a chalkboard, in two columns, the facts as presented in each of the Gospel passages. The following outline and questions might be helpful to the leader.

GOSPEL OF MATTHEW:

* Pilate sends guards as requested by Pharisees. (Why is this story presented?)

* Two women go to see the tomb. (Who are they?)

* Angel rolls away stone. (Who rolled away the stone in the Gospel of Mark?)

*Women run away. (Why?)

* Women and Jesus meet. (What does Jesus say to the women and what is their reaction?)

* Guards report body was stolen by disciples. (Why is this part of the narrative?)

GOSPEL OF LUKE:

* Women come with spices. (Are they named?)

* They find the stone rolled away. (How was the stone moved?)

* They enter the tomb and find no body.

* They find two men in shining garments. (Who are they?)

* They leave and tell the eleven disciples. (Does finding an empty tomb bring faith?)

* The disciples do not believe the women.

3. Spend a few minutes discussing how faith is arrived at in the Gospel of Luke. Again the following outline may be helpful:

— Road to Emmaus experience

— Eyes of the disciples ARE OPENED and they recognize Jesus. (What does this mean?)

— He immediately vanishes.

— Jesus appears to Peter.

— Conviction has been produced through the SEEING of Jesus.

4. Conclude the session with the class discussing the following questions:

A. How do you think Peter felt when he knew Jesus had risen, since he had been unfaithful to him when he was arrested? What would your feelings be?

B. If you were one of the persons on the road to Emmaus and Jesus had appeared to you, how would you report the event to your friends who are not followers of Jesus? Do you think your friends would find it difficult to believe? If so, why?

C. Do you believe it would be enough for you to know Jesus as a great teacher, as a person who helped persons, but who was crucified for his concern and efforts? What difference does it make to you that you have heard the news from Jesus' followers, "Jesus is risen! He lives!"

SESSION IV

There are four resurrection appearances in the Gospel of John. The first three take place near Jerusalem while the fourth, which seems to be an appendix to this Gospel, is in Galilee. First, Jesus appears to Mary Magdalene near the tomb on the first day of the week. That same evening he appears to ten of the disciples and eight days later he appears to all eleven disciples. The fourth appearance is some time later and is at the Sea of Galilee.

The longest account deals with Peter and Mary Magdalene. Mary goes early on the first day of the week to the tomb and discovers it has been opened. Mary hurries to tell Peter and the beloved disciple that someone has taken the body of Jesus. Peter and the beloved disciple run to the tomb. The other disciple arrives first, but only looks into the tomb. Moments later Peter arrives and enters the tomb and sees not only the cloths but the napkin which had been used to wrap the head, rolled up in a place by itself. Take note of the great detail in the narrative to the linen cloths. The mention of the cloths so neatly folded throws doubt on Mary's statement that Jesus had been taken someplace else. When the other disciple enters the tomb he sees and believes. He is the first person to accept the resurrection event. This is in keeping with his prominence throughout the Gospel of John.

The two disciples return home but Mary stays at the tomb crying. Later she looks into the tomb and sees two white angels. The idea of angels as messengers of God is clear but the actuality of conversation with them is difficult for modern readers. The two in white ask Mary why she is crying and she replies, "They have taken my Lord away, and I do not know where they have laid him." With this she turns around and sees Jesus but thinks him to be the gardener who has taken the body elsewhere. When Jesus speaks Mary's name, she realizes who it is. Jesus gives two commands to Mary — not to touch him and to go tell the others that he is returning to be with the Father.

The second appearance takes place that same evening before ten of the disciples who have gathered in some secret place. Even though the door is shut and locked, Jesus comes and appears among the ten disciples. The writer does not attempt to explain how Jesus rose from the tomb nor how he enters this room where the disciples are. Jesus shows the ten his hands and his side and they rejoice because they know it is Jesus. After they recognize him, he commissions them to go out as his spokesmen.

This third appearance takes place several days later and centers around the doubts of the disciple Thomas who had not been present at the first appearance of Jesus. Thomas would not accept the statement of the ten and Mary, "We have seen the Lord." At this gathering of the eleven Jesus again comes through the locked doors and stands before the ten and Thomas. Thomas is offered the oppurtunity he has requested, to touch the wounds of Jesus, to assure his faith. The words of Jesus seem to be sufficient to Thomas who now believes in the resurrection event.

SUGGESTED PROCEDURE

1. Each person should have a Bible available — preferably several different versions of the Bible should be available. First have one person read aloud John 20:1-29 to the whole group. Second, the class should divide into small study groups and assign one or two, depending on the size of the total group, of the following passages to study in depth: John 20:1-10, 11-18, 19-23, 24-25, 26-29. Each person should prepare a brief statement as to the insight they gain concerning the resurrection event after studying their assigned passage. These statements should be presented to the whole group.

2. List on the chalkboard the facts as presented in the Gospel of John. The following statements may be helpful:

— Body prepared before burial. (John 19:38-42)

— Mary Magdalene comes to visit the tomb.

— Mary finds the huge stone rolled away.

— Mary runs to Peter.

— Peter is the first witness of the Easter event (priority of Peter's faith).

— Grave cloths in orderly fashion (body was not stolen!).

— Jesus appears and speaks to Mary (Jesus sparks off the recognition).

— "Touch me not" (does this agree with other gospels?).

— Jesus appears to the ten disciples the same evening.

— Jesus enters through a locked door.

— Jesus appears a few days later to the ten disciples plus the doubting Thomas.

(Gospel of John originally finished after the Thomas story. John 21, it is assumed, was written by a different author.)

3. Spend time comparing the outlines of the four gospels, discussing the similarities and differences which seem to appear. Spend a few minutes discussing whether or not the group believes any of the writers were eyewitnesses to any of the events presented in their writings.

4. This session might conclude with a conversation centering around this faith statement:

The words of Thomas are not final ones because his faith had been established by actual sight. The last words belong to Jesus who questions the doubting Thomas about his triumphant belief based on sight and sound so that he will not think it is the ultimate level of religious life. The highest blessing comes to those who, like the beloved disciple, possess an insight which surpasses the senses. "Blessed are those who have NOT seen and yet believe."

Children's Activities

ONLY KINGS RIDE COLTS

by Janice Bacon

It was hot that morning in Bethany. Reuben had finished his chores with the animals and was ready to go back into the house to see if he was needed any more. He and his friend, Samuel had planned to go into Jerusalem for the rest of the day. It was Passover time and hundreds of people were arriving in the city every day for the holidays. Inn keepers hired boys to bring travelers to their Inns. Reuben and Samuel had already worked two days that week and the Inn keepers promised them two more days' work if they could get into the city. The work was not hard, it was fun and the boys were able to earn a few cents as well.

As Reuben came around the corner of his house, he heard what sounded like a crowd of people. It looked like they were heading toward Jerusalem. They were still a way off, but while he watched the crowd stopped and the leaders were talking among themselves. Then several of the strangers left the crowd and came toward his house. As they neared, Reuben could tell that they were not from his area. They were dusty and looked as though they had traveled a long way.

"Friend, we have need of your colt," one of the men said to Reuben. One of the men began untying the colt before Reuben could answer.

"But, sir," said Reuben, "my father is in the house and I must ask him."

Reuben ran into the house quickly and called his father. "Father, some strangers are here and they want to take our colt!"

Joash, Reuben's father, hurried to the door. "Why do you take my colt?"

"Our Lord has need of it," they replied.

"Take it, then."

Reuben could not believe his ears! His father was letting these strangers take a new colt, one that had never been ridden. And his father did not seem worried or concerned. He even looked sort of proud. Reuben wondered what was going on.

When the men left, taking the colt back to the waiting crowd, Reuben said, "Father, Samuel and I are going into the city now. We will be home before dark."

Reuben could hardly wait to tell Samuel about the strangers. He hurried to find his friend. He knew Samuel would be just as anxious as he was to follow the parade to Jerusalem.

The road from Bethany down the Mount of Olives to Jerusalem was a rocky one. The crowd surrounding the man on the donkey colt was first running ahead of him then following and sometimes pressing close to him. It was an incredible scene. The closer they came to Jerusalem, the more excited the crowd became. Someone had put a cloak over the donkey's back for the men to sit on. Now, people were beginning to lay their cloaks on the road for the donkey to walk on. All along the way, more people joined the parade as it moved through the village. They shouted, "Praise God who sends David's son!", "Hail to the King!", "Praise Him who comes in the name of the Lord!"

Samuel and Reuben ran through clouds of dust to catch up to the parade. They heard snatches of the shouting, "Lord" and "King", and they wondered who the people were shouting about.

"Reuben, who was that, anyway? The man who wanted your colt?"

"I don't know. But all those people are saying something about a King. You know that only Kings ride on colts, so this man must be King!"

The two boys were able to run faster than the crowd could, so they were soon out in front of the mob. Someone had cut branches off trees and was spreading them along the rocky, dusty road. Samuel and Reuben picked up branches, too, and began to wave them. "Hosanna", they shouted with all the others. "Hosanna!"

Samuel and Reuben made their way easily down the rocky road toward Jerusalem. They waved their branches and shouted "Hosanna! Make way for the King!"

They could see the city ahead, its golden domes glistening in the bright sun. Dust rose around their feet as they hurried along. When they reached the outskirts of the city, the boys stopped in the shade of the Zusan Gate to wait for the crowd to catch up. People gathered at the gate to watch the parade winding down the steep hill. It was a sight to behold! The calm, quiet man riding a colt seemed to be all alone even though he was in the middle of a shouting, happy mob of people. The man seemed to be unaware of the noise.

The crowd seemed to grow quieter as they neared Jerusalem. The people dropped behind the man on the colt to let him enter the great city of Jerusalem first. Reuben and Samuel stood aside near the gateway to the city. As the man reached the boys, he allowed the colt to stop. He looked at Reuben and said, "Your colt has made my journey easier today. He was calm in the crowd and surefooted on the rocky road. He will be remembered." The man smiled at Reuben, nodded slightly, then let the colt move on through the Zusan Gate into the city. The crowd of people, now very large and very loud, followed him.

Many days later, Samuel and Reuben were to remember that day and talk about it over and over again. They would talk about the great crowd of people who spread palm branches on the road. They would remember the loud "Hosannas" they shouted. But most of all, they would talk about the man on the colt. They would tell of his kind eyes, his sad smile and the way he sat on that colt as he entered Jerusalem; truly like a King!

THE LIFE OF CHRIST

by Colleen Britton

The excitement of Christmas was over and our "Juniors" church school class was beginning a new unit — THE LIFE OF JESUS. The study followed the events in Jesus' life from his birth to resurrection. We were searching for some large project which would emphasize the greatness of Christ's life and at the same time would help reinforce what the children would learn as the unit progressed.

"What if we produced our own filmstrip as a class project?" The idea was enthusiastically received by both class and teachers.

After watching and carefully evaluating two filmstrips on the "Life of Jesus," the youngsters wrote an outline of his life which included events, miracles, and teachings. From this outline small groups began research in the Gospels, Bible Atlas, Bible Encyclopedia, and other books. They compressed their research on each topic into brief paragraphs which later served as a script. Their enthusiasm mounted as the work continued. Many volunteered to work on their topics at home and brought back pages *they* had typed and art work *they* had done to use as illustrations. Their enthusiasm also produced considerable interest in the project from parents who were pleasantly surprised to see their children working on a church school project at home during the week.

As research progressed, there were many opportunities to discuss: "What was Jesus trying to teach us through this particular parable?" "Why did this happen?" "How would you have reacted if you had been there?" "What does this mean to us today?" Many of our discussions found their way into the narrative. The finished script was nearly twelve typewritten pages long, and it took several sessions for the children to record it.

Pictures were gathered from church school files, Christmas cards, magazines, and books. Illustrations were found for each event. The children photographed them with a close-up lens. Their original art work was also photographed and used for some of the illustrations.

After nearly three months of work, the project was shared with the congregation at an evening fellowship dinner. It was also shown to other church school classes and to the parents after the Sunday morning worship service. Popcorn was even served at one of the showings. The slide/tape presentation was enjoyed by all. The children listened and watched intently. They were quick to point out,"That's me talking," "I drew that one," and "I took that picture." The parents and other members of the congregation applauded the achievement.

Even more important, the children really did learn about Christ's life and teachings. They were totally involved in the learning process through reading, researching, drawing, writing, photographing it, listening, discussing, and seeing. Children remember what they DO, and they will long remember "The Life of Jesus."

The completed tape and slide tray have also become a permanent Christian education resource which can be used again to help other groups know of Jesus Christ.

A SHARING CONVERSATION WITH YOUNG CHILDREN

by Robert G. Davidson

This lesson plan can be used as a part of a church school class session. It has been designed to draw children and teachers into a conversational sharing time.

Jesus' resurrection is a sign of new life. Spring and Easter promise new life for all of us. Discovering new life, new possibilities in the springtime is exciting, because new opportunities, beauty and love make us happy. We all feel a great joy and happiness at Easter as we come to know that Jesus is with us.

As adults we might like to have less emphasis placed on Easter bunnies and their generosity, but we must use the children's experience to advantage. Eggs are signs of new life and we should relate this to our discussion of Easter. If children receive new clothes or shoes at Easter, these too are signs of change and new beginnings in a sense.

Perhaps as adults we need to remember that the most important part of the day for children is the moment of spontaneous celebration they express when they discover their Easter basket from the Easter bunny. The great shouts of joy, the beating of the heart, and the wide smiles on the faces express the wonder of discovery; that is what Easter is all about. Jesus is with us! Hallelujah!

So we might do better if we do not try to dispel the magical concept, just accept the child's point of view. In time, children who have been introduced to the story of Jesus and who sense faith lived out by the adults around them, will grow to an understanding of the Easter event and the great mystery which surrounds it.

Spend a few minutes talking to the children about the story of Jesus and his resurrection. As you talk about the story, some of the children may raise questions which are difficult for you to answer. It may be necessary to give the simple but honest answer "I am not sure about that." Such an answer allows for future study. You may wish to spend time at this point talking about mysteries and secrets, making it clear that our understanding is still incomplete. We have nothing to fear in being honest with young children. Make this a time of sharing the great joy of the Easter event! RGD

THE CUSTOMS OF LENT

by Elaine M. Ward

The customs of Lent seem strange to today's Christians. If we saw a man dressed in metal armor or a woman in the skins of an animal, we would be curious, just as we are curious about the customs of Lent in the past.

Within the armor or the skin, the man and the woman, however, would be much like you and me, with some of the same thoughts and feelings and wishes. Behind the Lenten customs, the symbols, stand some of the same reality and meaning we look for today and which people will continue to look for tomorrow.

Lent consists of 40 days (not including Sundays which were known as "little Easter") before Easter, representing the 40 days and nights Jesus spent in the wilderness without food. The early church remembered this time by "fasting," going without food, usually that meant. In time the custom changed; going without food was the way Jesus wanted to concentrate only on being alone with God, depending solely on God. Many people give up something in order to remember and to show their dependence upon God. This act is even more meaningful when what is given up is shared with others in the form of food or clothing or money.

On Ash Wednesday, the first day of Lent, palm branches are burned and the ashes used to make the sign of the cross on the foreheads of the worshipers. The day before, however, is a festive, "fat" day of rejoicing, especially in eating the food one would not be allowed during Lent and thus was called "fat" Tuesday or Mardi Gras.

The events of Holy Week consist of Palm Sunday and Jesus' entry into Jerusalem. "Maundy Thursday," the night of the Last Supper when Jesus sent Peter and John to find and prepare a room for their meal together, comes from the first word of an ancient Latin hymn sung on this day, "Mandatum novum do vobis" or "A new commandment I give you" (John 13:34).

Christians continue the tradition begun that night when they celebrate the Lord's Supper or Communion in the eating of bread and wine in remembrance of that event and in participating in the forgiveness of God.

In Germany the day is called Green Thursday and a green branch is given as a sign that their Lenten penance is completed. Throughout Europe this Thursday is called "holy" Thursday or "sheer" Thursday, meaning "clean", in reference to the washing of the church altar on that day. During the Middle Ages the kings of England always washed the feet of the poor, as Jesus did in John 13:1-5.

It's the "Lord's Supper"
Please come in.
Everyone's ready,
Time to begin.
"This is my body,"
Jesus said.
"Given for you," As he broke the bread.
"This is the blood of the covenant,
Drink it up,"
Jesus said,
As he took the cup.
"This is my promise.
This is my vow.
I'll be with you always,
As I'm with you now.
This is my promise,
This is my plea,
Drink of my cup
And eat with me
Now and forever
Through eternity."

91

"Good" Friday is a dark, discouraging day in the church. It is "God's" day and it is good only in the sense that Christ's mission is completed in his crucifixion on a cross. As a child, I remember spending the three hours from 12 to 3 p.m., in a darkened church, hearing his last words. The cross was covered in black, the color of grief and sadness.

> *At his death the world grew dark, the curtain covering*
> *The holy of holies was split in two.*
> *They nailed him to a cross in Golgotha,*
> *"Place of the skull," and left him there to die,*
> *Remembering the paid and angry crowd*
> *In Pilate's court and their inhuman cry, "Crucify!"*
> *Between two thieves he hung, "King of the Jews,"*
> *On that Good Friday when the day turned night*
> *Inside the topsy-turvy world where God*
> *Would once again, in love, on Easter Day,*
> *Make all things right!*

Easter is a day of joy and celebration in the Christian church. Its color is white for new life and purity, for the victory of God. Easter says that sorrow can turn to joy, that nothing in the world is so powerful or evil that it can stop God's love for us. Christ is risen...God is with us!

Flowers and food are used to remind us of God's victory and love. Lovely, white, bell-like lilies announce this victory in church and home.

The egg was used as such a symbol of new life, for within the egg is life itself. The shell was also thought of as the rock tomb from which Christ emerged. Around the world eggs are colored and decorated and enjoyed. In Greece, or wherever there are members of the Greek Orthodox faith, hard boiled eggs are dyed red to represent the blood of Christ, which are ceremoniously cracked on Easter day to symbolize the resurrection and the freeing of the Spirit of Christ.

The Easter "bunny" or rabbit is a symbol of the season because of its fertility. Even clothing reminds us, as worshipers wear new clothes, as the newly baptized Christians chose to wear white linen to symbolize "new" life. Activities at Easter include:

1. Look at pictures of symbols, such as "butterfly," waves around eggs standing for eternity, a cross, trinity, JC, Savior, talk about and draw them.

2. Dye and paint eggs with symbols. Hard cook the eggs. Chill them. Dry thoroughly. Using a fine paintbrush and liquid rubber cement, paint designs on the eggs. Let the cement dry completely. Dye the eggs in vegetable dyes, available at food stores. When the shell has been dyed, roll it across several thicknesses of paper towel so that the excess color is also absorbed. Dry and rub off the rubber cement.

3. Make a cross from two sticks and decorate it with live flowers. You might want to make arrangements or visit the sanctuary or an elderly church school class, singing Easter songs and sharing one of the crosses.

4. Fill in the following: Lent is_____. People waved _____ on Palm Sunday. We celebrate Easter because _____. A cross is symbol of _____. "Maundy" means _____. A symbol for Easter is _____.

5. Do an Easter Crossword. Find the following words: Easter, cross, allelu, lives, joy, love, die:

A	L	L	E	L	U
B	X	C	D	I	E
I	J	R	Y	V	Z
E	L	O	V	E	E
N	A	S	Y	S	L
E	A	S	T	E	R

6. Make Hot Cross Buns throughout the Lenten season. You will need: 1 box Hot Roll mix, 1/3 cup sugar, ½ cup seedless raisins, ¼ teaspoon allspice, 1 teaspoon cinnamon. Prepare Hot Roll mix as directed on the package. Add the other ingredients, divide, and shape into buns. Bake as directed on the package. Mix 1 cup confectioners sugar, 2 teaspoons water, 2 tablespoons melted butter together. Add more sugar if necessary and make a cross on each bun.

7. Make Easter cards from colorful gift wrapping paper. Cut the paper into 5" x 6" and fold in half. Write a message or Bible verse on a piece of white paper or index card and paste it to the inside of the paper. Young children may draw or "scribble" a message.

92

REMEMBERING PALM SUNDAY

by Colleen Britton

There are only a few more days left until Passover, and everyone is talking about Jesus of Nazareth. Will he come defiantly into Jerusalem? Will he finally restore the kingdom of Israel? What new miracles will he perform? There are stories that he can raise the dead. He is greatly feared by the authorities and they would like to have him arrested. Do you think he will risk coming to Jerusalem for Passover, or do you think he will stay in Galilee where he is safe and can preach freely?

The word spreads like wildfire that first Palm Sunday morning. "He is coming!" the crowds rush out and line the narrow road from Bethany trying to catch a glimpse of Jesus. "The king is coming!" "Hosanna!" "Hosanna!" "Save us, Jesus!" Shouts echo for miles. Palm branches are hastely cut and placed on the ground in front of him in his honor. Slowly Jesus rides by the crowds, not on a horse as would a mighty king, but on a donkey, a sign that he comes in peace. "Oh, this will surely be a week to be remembered. God's kingdom will surely be restored. Hallelujah!"

How can we help our children and congregation share in the experience of that first Palm Sunday? Dramatize the event! A simple line drawing of Jesus riding on a donkey is traced onto a transparency and projected onto a large piece of cardboard with an overhead projector. The almost lifesize figure is then cut out and painted on both sides with poster paint by the children. This can be done during church school or as part of an activity center during Lenten workshop. The events leading up to Palm Sunday and the feelings of the crowds are discussed. Make use of available pictures, filmstrips, books, etc. Role play the events with the young people several times to allow them to identify with the various characters' feelings: Jesus, disciples, crowds, priests.

With the children, plan a Palm Sunday "Mini Pageant". Real palm branches can be cut and loosely tied to the ends of each row of pews in the sanctuary. At a prearranged signal near the end of the morning worship service, costumed children line the center aisle and hold the palm branches. Questions are asked by several children, "Do you think he will come to Jerusalem?" "Where is he?" etc. Suddenly from the rear of the sanctuary are shouts of, "He's coming!" "Jesus is coming!" "Hail the king!" "Hosanna!" "Hosanna!" Jesus and the donkey are slowly led to the front of the sanctuary as palm branches are set down before him. Children in the rear of the sanctuary follow the procession and crowd around Jesus at the front of the church where a loud unison shout of "Hosanna!" is heard. A rousing Palm Sunday hymn is sung by the whole congregation, and the service and dramatization end with a prayer.

As we continue to share our children's learning experiences with the entire congregation, we are enriching both. The children's spontaneity gives a special life to any worship service, and by sharing their experiences with others, they reinforce and remember what they learn. So, relive and share the Palm Sunday experience with your congregation this year.

THE EMPTY TOMB

by Steven Edwards

(An echo pantomime based on John 20:1-10)
John was one of the twelve disciples of Jesus. In fact, Jesus loved John very dearly. We are going to tell a story about how John's sadness was turned into joy. You repeat everything I say and everything I do – just like and echo.

WORDS	ACTIONS
My name is John	*stand straight, point thumb to chest*
I am the disciple Jesus loved	*hug yourself, twisting from side to side at the waist*
Three days after Jesus died	*hold up three fingers*
I was very sad	*frown*
And tired	*droop shoulders and sigh*
Because I hadn't slept much	*rest head on hands*
None of us knew what to do	*arms down, palms forward, shake head*
It was just before sunrise	*arms out to side, palms moving upward*
When Mary walked to his tomb	*slap one thigh then the other (3 or 4 times)*
The stone door had been rolled away	*roll hands over each other*
And Mary was frightened	*pull shoulders in, hold hands in front of face*
So she ran away from the tomb	*rapidly slap one thigh then the other*
She kept on running	*keep slapping*
And she ran some more	*keep slapping*
When she saw Peter and me	*still slapping*
She stopped	*stop slapping*
"Someone has taken the Lord's body."	*wave arms in the air*
"We don't know where he is."	*shake head*
Before she said anything else	*stand straight*
Peter ran toward the tomb	*rapidly slap one thigh then the other*
Then I ran after him	*keep slapping*
Soon I passed him up	*still slapping, look over shoulder*
And went to the tomb	*keep slapping*
But I didn't go in	*stop slapping*
I was frightened, too	*pull in shoulders, hold hands in front of face*
Peter ran right inside	*rapidly slap one thigh then the other*
He saw Jesus' clothes lying flat on the table	*move hands parallel to the floor in opposite directions with palms down*
And off to one side	*point to the side*
His head band was rolled up	*roll up head band*
Then I slowly walked inside	*slowly slap one thigh then the other*
Peter looked at me	*look to one side*
And I looked at Peter	*look to the other side*
Then we both smiled	*smile*
I said, "No one has taken his body."	*shake head*
"Jesus is alive again."	*arms up*
Peter nodded his head	*nod head*
Then we hugged each other	*hug yourself*
And went back to tell the others the good news	*slap one thigh and then the other*
So, my friends	*point forward*
Whenever we are sad	*frown*
And you don't know what to do	*arms down, palms forward, shake head*
Remember this	*point to forehead*
What may look very bad	*stand straight*
Could turn out to be something good	*fold arms across chest*

THE NEWS OF THE DAY
30 A.D.

BETRAYAL AND ARREST
(On-the-spot interview)

by Jane Priewe

Characters: Isaac (Man announcer), Miriam (Woman announcer), Captain, Jesus, Judas, Malchus, Peter (for action only if presented before an audience).

Sound effects: Marching feet and muttering voices (softly in background), metal against metal (to sound like spears striking against armor), scuffling sounds (for when Peter cuts off Malchus' ear).

This interview-type presentation can be taped for listening, or it can be presented by live actors and actresses in front of an audience.

Isaac: Ladies and gentlemen, this is Isaac, your L E N T reporter. We interrupt Midnight Mood Music to bring you special on-the-spot coverage of an arrest. While I see if I can find the Roman captain for an interview, will you describe what's happening, Miriam?

Miriam: I'll do my best, Isaac, It's a dark night, folks, and you can probably hear the shuffle and stomp of marching feet in the background. A Roman captain is leading the garrison of about five hundred men out of Jerusalem. The high priest has sent men along with the Roman soldiers to support them on this dangerous mission. We have just passed through the East Gate, and are moving swiftly along the Kedron Road toward the Mount of Olives. Lanterns and torches, carried by soldiers, twinkle and gleam in the darkness, and we can hear spears and armor clanks as the soldiers march. It is...

Isaac: Excuse me, Miriam. The captain says he'll give me a quick interview before we reach our destination. (Sound of marching feet and metal against metal a bit louder) You say this is a dangerous mission, captain?

Captain: I assume so, or I would not have been ordered to bring a full cohort of soldiers. All I've been told is that fellow over there will show me the man I am to arrest.

Isaac: Who is the fellow, captain?

Captain: Not a very shining example, I'm afraid. His name is Judas, and I understand he's been traveling with the man I'm to arrest. I'd say he's a betrayer, wouldn't you?

Isaac: Indeed I would! Look down the road, Captain! Are those men coming toward us in the distance?

Captain: One of them could be the criminal I'm after. I must return to my station.

Isaac: Thank you, for sparing me time for an interview, sir. Miriam, have you anything to report?

Miriam: I've moved closer to the leaders, Isaac. There's a man they call Judas near me. He's talking to Malchus, a slave of the high priest. I just heard Judas say the sign would be a kiss, but I don't understand what he means, so I'll stay close to him. Some men are approaching us. The man Judas is going up to...Isaac! It's the same man we saw make a shambles of the temple on Monday. The one called Jesus! I'll try to get close enough to pick up their conversation.

Jesus: Judas, are you betraying the Son of Man with a kiss?

Judas: Rabbi. (Kisses Jesus)

(Sound of scuffle in interview for listening. For watching, soldiers grasp Jesus' arms. He does not resist. Peter draws sword and cuts off Malchus' right ear. Malchus clutches head, and yells. Jesus touches the ear and heals it. Use this bit of action only if presented in front of an audience.)

Jesus: Put your sword away, Peter! Those who use the sword shall die by the sword. Don't you know I could call to my Father for help, and He'd send thousands of angels? It must happen this way, so that the scriptures can be fulfilled! (Turns from Peter to the crowd of people) Why do you come with swords and clubs to arrest me like a common robber? I used to teach you in the temple, and you didn't seize me then.

(Disciples run away)

Miriam: Jesus is being led away by soldiers, Isaac. The men who were with him have run away. You! Slave!

Malchus: Me, ma'am?

Miriam: Yes, you. Would you tell me your name? I know you are a slave of Caiaphas, the high priest.

Malchus: Yes, ma'am. My name is Malchus.

Miriam: Could you tell our listening audience what happened between you and the man with the sword?

Malchus: He's one of those fellows following the Nazarene. I think his name is Peter. He nearly sliced my right ear off with a sword!

Miriam: Oh, come now! Your ear looks all right to me.

Malchus: Well, I *know* I felt the blade, and I thought my head was going to go, but the one called Jesus touched my ear, and now it's okay. I don't understand any of this, ma'am. I gotta' go. The high priest will have me whipped, if I don't report back to him.

Miriam: Thanks for giving me this much of your time. Isaac, have you any more interviews?

Isaac: No, Miriam. The crowd is following the soldiers back to Jerusalem. Thank you folks for listening to another on-the-spot interview.

THE CRUCIFIXION
(On-the-spot interview)

Characters: Isaac (Man reporter), Miriam (Woman reporter), 1st Thief, 2nd Thief, Jesus, Centurion, Mary, Jew.

Props: Three crosses made from styrofoam of left-over lumber, sign for Jesus' cross, sponge or the end of a stick. No props are needed if this interview-type play is taped or done on a microphone behind screens.

Isaac: This Passover Festival has really been an exciting one, and Station L E N T is bringing you on-the-spot coverage of the unexpected trouble which has plagued Jerusalem ever since the man called Jesus of Nazareth made his triumphant entry last Sunday. This morning Miriam and I are covering the crucifixion of two robbers and Jesus. The three men have been nailed to crosses. Miriam can you give our listeners a description of where we are while I find someone to interview?

Miriam: We're located just outside of Jerusalem's North wall, near the Damascus gate. We are on a rocky ledge some thirty feet above Jeremiah's Grotto, and the hill looks like a skull. The Romans call the hill Calvary. Crucifixion is the Roman way of punishing slaves, criminals, and foreigners. I'm told it is a most painful death. Nails are driven through the victim's hands and feet, and he's left on the cross to suffer starvation, thirst, and constant agony. It generally takes from four to six days for death to come. This...

Isaac: May I break in, Miriam? I'm at the base of the middle cross, and a centurion has agreed to talk with me. Your name, sir?

Centurion: Horatius. Make it snappy, will you? We're going to gamble for the Galilean's clothes, and I'd like to win his robe. It's a fine piece of fabric. There's not a seam in it!

Isaac: I'll be as brief as possible Horatius. What time did you bring these three criminals to Calvary?

Centurion: About nine o'clock this morning.

Isaac: What was the first thing you did?

Centurion: Well, you gotta' get them up on the crosses, you know.

Isaac: Do you give the men anything to deaden the pain?

Centurion: Sure! You think we're animals? We offer wine mixed with gall. Both the thieves took it, but the Galilean refused. Never saw such self-control! While we were nailing him to the cross, he said, "Father, forgive them: they don't know what they're doing." Or something like that. If *I* was being nailed up there, you wouldn't hear me asking *my* dad to forgive anyone!

Isaac: The sign on the middle cross hanging over the Nazarene's head, whose idea was that?

Centurion: Our noble governor, Pontius Pilate, wrote: "Jesus The Nazarene, The King of the Jews." He wrote it in Latin, Greek, and Hebrew so everyone could read it. Say, fellow, you will have to excuse me. Looks like the boys are ready to cast lots for the clothes.

Isaac: Thanks for the interview, Horatius.

Miriam: Isaac, can you hear me? Am I coming through?

Isaac: Loud and clear, Miriam. What's all the shouting in the background?

Miriam: The crowd of people gathered here is taunting and shouting at the Galilean.

Isaac: Do you recognize any of the people in the crowd?

Miriam: Almost all of them, Isaac. Chief priests, scribes, Jewish elders, and even some Romans are jeering at Jesus. Oh, what a hard-hearted, inhuman crowd they are! They have no compassion for these men, suffering on the crosses.

Isaac: What are they shouting, Miriam?

Miriam: An elder just yelled, "If you can destroy and rebuild the temple in three days, save yourself! If you're the Son of God, come down from the cross!"

Isaac: Brutal! Heartless!

Miriam: One of the high priests has pushed closer to shout, "He saved others, but he can't save himself! If he's the King of Israel, let him come down from the cross, and I'll believe him." Oh, Isaac, this is too sad! Now, one of the thieves on the other cross is taunting the poor man!

Isaac: This is a far cry from the royal welcome these people gave the Galilean when he entered Jerusalem last Sunday. Hold on a minute, Miriam. I think I'm close enough to the crosses to pick up any words the crucified men might say. Listen!

1st Thief: Hey, fellow! Aren't you the Christ? If you are, how about saving yourself and us, too?

2nd Thief: Don't talk like that! Have you no fear of God? Man, we deserve our sentences, because we're robbers, but this Nazarene has not done a thing wrong to deserve treatment like this! Will you remember me when you come into your kingdom, Jesus?

Jesus: Truly, I say to you, today you'll be with me in Paradise.

Miriam: Isaac, I've found a small group of grieving women here, now that the priests and their followers have been shoved back by soldiers.

Isaac: Who are the women, Miriam? Find out what you can about them.

Miriam: What is your name, please?

Mary: I'm Mary, the wife of Clopas.

Miriam: And these other women, who are they?

Mary: One is Mary Magdalene, a follower of Jesus. The other is Mary, his mother.

Miriam: Mother! Jesus' mother? How terrible that she must see this dreadful thing happening to her son! Who is the young man standing near the mother?

Mary: That's John, one of the Zebedee boys. He's a follower of Jesus, too.

Miriam: Look! Jesus has found the strength to raise his head! He's looking at his mother.

Jesus: Woman, behold your son! John behold your mother!

Miriam: What on earth does he mean?

97

Mary: That John should take Jesus' place, and treat Mary as though she were his own mother. And he'll do it, too! You can depend on it. Oh, my goodness, what's happening now?

(Distant thunder)

Miriam: It's getting darker, and it's only noon! Isaac, are you still near the crosses? Has anything happened there?

Isaac: No, Miriam, although this darkness puzzles me. It's nearly as dark as night. The man Jesus is quiet, but I can tell he's suffering a great deal. Wait! He's speaking!

Jesus: My God, my God, why have You forsaken me?

Jew: He's calling for Elijah!

Jesus: I'm thirsty.

Isaac: Horatius is offering Jesus sour wine on a sponge hooked to the end of a long reed.

Jesus: (Cries out) It is finished!

Isaac: Jesus is dead, Miriam!

Miriam: The earth is shaking, Isaac! And there's loud thunder and terrible lightning! I've never seen weather like this. It frightens me!

Isaac: Everyone is frightened, Miriam. Horatius! Centurion! Why are you kneeling at the foot of the middle cross?

Horatius: I just saw a rock crack right in half! I don't know what to make of this! It's scary! Great Caesar's ghost! I really think this man Jesus is the Son of God!

JESUS IS RISEN
(Character study)

Characters: Soldier, Angel, Mary Magdalene, Simon Peter

This character study can be presented any number of ways. If done in a room, block off each corner with a sheet or screen, and let a character step from behind his or her screen at the proper time. Sheet draped costumes would add a great deal to the presentation.

You could use the door idea from the 'Laugh-In' television show. Make one or two doors in a large piece of cardboard, and have each character open a door at the appropriate time. No costumes are needed here, because only the shoulders and head show in the opening, but special head coverings could be used to help characterize the actors. The angel would have a gold and silver halo over his head. The soldier could wear a foil covered helmet, easily made by covering a paper bag with aluminum foil and shaping to look like a helmet. Mary wears a simple draped head covering, and Peter, a colorful striped towel pinned into a close fitting head covering with the excess hanging over his shoulders and back.

Soldier: My name is Flavius, and I'm one of the soldiers ordered by the high priests to guard Jesus's tomb. Everything went quietly on Saturday after the priests sealed the tomb. It was about the most pleasant assignment I'd had in a long time, because the garden was shady and cool, and it smelled nice from all the flowers blooming. We soldiers took turns spelling each other, so there was always one guard on watch, and often there were two of us. Well, early Sunday morning, the first day of the Jewish week, the earth shook and rumbled. It had done the same thing Friday afternoon when the Nazarene died, but this time I was *really* scared! Man! I was *so* scared, I could not *move*! Then this stranger appeared from somewhere. His face was as blinding as bright lightning, and his robes were whiter than snow. It hurt my eyes to look at him! Even more frightening, the stone the high priests had sealed over the tomb's opening, moved away from the tomb! As soon as I could move, I ran all the way to the high priests palace in Jerusalem. I told Caiaphas what had happened. I figured he would lay a really heavy punishment on us for leaving the garden with the tomb unguarded, but he gave each of us soldiers a lot of money just to say the disciples had stolen Jesus away at night while we slept. Not a whit of truth in it, of course, but we took the money, and spread the lie all over the city.

Angel: I am an angel sent by God to help the Savior. My job was to get a message to the disciples and let everyone know that Jesus had risen from the dead. The soldiers left to guard the sealed tomb were so frightened when I first appeared about sunrise, they stood like they were frozen. Finally, they ran away, and soon after that women came to the tomb. They carried spices and oils, I suppose for Jesus' body, since they had done such a rush job on Friday evening.

When the women saw me, they were frightened, too, but I reassured them, "Don't be afraid," I said. "I know you are looking for Jesus, but he is not here. He has risen. Come and see the place where he was lying." They looked at the linen wrappings.

"Go and tell his disciples that he is risen from the dead," I told them. "Jesus is going to Galilee, and will see you there."

The women hurried away to tell the disciples that Jesus' body was gone from the tomb. They were really very upset, but I suppose it was because they didn't understand what had happened.

Mary Magdalene: My name is Mary Magdalene, and I have loved and followed the Master ever since he cast seven demons from my body. Early Sunday morning just as day was breaking, I hurried with the other Mary and some women to the tomb where our Lord was buried. The sun was just up, birds were chirping, and a cool fragrance bathed the garden.

We had been talking about how we'd get the stone away from the tomb, because it was all Nicodemus and Joseph could do to move it in place on Friday evening. When we arrived at the tomb, we were surprised to find the stone not covering the entrance. We peered inside, and saw a young man dressed in dazzling white. Even though he told us not to be afraid, we were terrified! We kept our heads bowed, and listened while he said we should tell Peter and the other disciples that the Master had gone to Galilee, and would see us there. You can imagine how shocked we were to find Jesus' body gone, can't you? We were frantic to know what had become of him, so we ran to tell the disciples. Peter and John were as upset as we were when they heard what we had to tell. They ran to the tomb to see if what we said was the truth. I tried to keep up with them, but after running to where they were staying in Jerusalem, I was too out of breath to stay close to them. After Peter and John had seen that we were not lying to them, they left

the garden. I broke down and cried. My poor Lord! Who could have stolen his precious body? Where could he be? I stood outside the tomb weeping, and saw two white-clad men inside.

"Why are you crying?" one of them asked.

"Because someone has taken my Lord away, and I don't know where," I answered, turning away from the tomb to leave the garden.

A man stood near me, and I thought he might be a gardener. He asked me why I was crying and who I was looking for. I told him, "Jesus". Why I even accused that gardener of hiding the body. Then I almost fainted when the gardener's face and voice became Jesus'! I could hardly get to the disciples fast enough to tell them I had seen the Lord. Hallelujah! Jesus Is Risen!

Peter: My name is Simon Peter, and I had nothing to do with moving the Master's body from the tomb, even though soldiers have started rumors that we disciples took his body during the night. For goodness sake, we didn't even know the body was gone until Mary Magdalene and the other women ran all the way from the garden to tell us someone had hidden Jesus' body.

Young John Zebedee and I hurried to the tomb to see if Mary might be mistaken, because sometimes she does get a bit excited, but she had told it like it was. John's younger than I am, so he outran me, and got to the tomb first.

"Hurry up, Peter," he called, stooping to peer into the tomb. "I can see the linen wrappings that were around his body," he shouted.

John didn't go inside the tomb, but I did, and he was right! The linen wrappings were there, and the face cloth that had been on Jesus' head. The face cloth was not lying with the linen wrappings, but had been pushed aside.

John followed me into the tomb, and after he had seen the linen and face cloth close up, he got all excited. "I believe, Peter!" he yelled. "The Master has risen from the dead!"

I went away with John, wondering if what he believed was true. I wished I could feel as sure about it as young John, but by night I *was* convinced. I was *happy*. I was *positive* because by then, I'd actually seen Jesus. Hosanna! Christ *has* risen from the dead!

EASTER

by Rudy Thomas

During Lent Christian people are to make special efforts to learn more about God and Jesus and about themselves.

Did you do that? Did you learn more about God and Jesus—and about yourself in church school?

But now the Big Day is here—EASTER! Today all Christian people have a very special feeling because this is the day we celebrate the resurrection of Jesus.

It is difficult to understand what is meant when we talk about the resurrection. Well, I have news for you. I don't understand it all either. But what I do understand makes it the most wonderful day of the year. Today we don't see the risen Jesus walking around. But what we *can see* is the result of God's wonderful power right before our eyes.

Have you seen any flowers growing in your yard yet? If you have, they are probably crocuses, maybe even daffodils or jonquils, or perhaps tulips. In any case, these beautiful plants have been in the ground all winter long. Oh, we could not *see* them, but they were still there sleeping as it were. But then the warmer air and the rains came and wonder of wonder those plants shot up through the earth and *bloomed.*

Now that is *resurrection!* What *seemed* dead is now *alive!* These plants were *dead* so far as we could *see.* Right? In fact, we could not even see the bulbs because they were buried in the ground. We could not *see* for *looking.* This reminds us that resurrection means God's power at work in His world. We cannot see that power, but we see the *results* of God's power in the beautiful flowers.

A few minutes ago we all heard the story of the resurrection of Jesus as we find it in the Bible. We cannot tell exactly what happened that first Easter morning but something wonderful happened for we are told that the tomb that held the body of Jesus was found to be empty. Jesus just was not in that tomb anymore.

A resurrected Jesus will not do us any good unless we get him inside ourselves. When we let Jesus live in our hearts then we know the miracle of the resurrection.

And now I want to read for you a few lines from the Bible ("The Song of Solomon" 2:11-12a):

> "For lo, the winter is past, the rain is over and gone.
> The flowers appear on the earth,
> *the time of singing has come.*"

The "time of singing has come" again. I want you to join with the whole congregation as we sing an Easter song that tells us just how Jesus can be alive today. Let's really sing it like we mean it:

> "He lives, he lives, Jesus Christ lives today. . .
> You ask me how I know he lives?
> HE LIVES WITHIN MY HEART!"

HOLY WEEK DISPLAYS
A Lenten Study

by Colleen Britton

We remember what we do, and what we discover, for ourselves. As children become involved in the study of Holy Week, either individually or in small groups, they will remember what they learn. The following work sheets can be adapted to each Holy Week event and used by both individual students or small groups. This lenten study can be used effectively with juniors/primaries and even jr. highs during church school class or youth group meetings. The finished displays can be shared with the congregation after services on Palm Sunday, at a Maundy Thursday service, or other Lenten family gathering.

NOTE: Collect "teaching pictures" of the Holy Week events from your church library or resource center. Magazines and old curriculum can also be used. Score (cut halfway through) cardboard from large appliance cartons to make folding, freestanding display boards about 3' high by 4' wide. These can be saved and used as teaching resources in the future.

EVENTS OF HOLY WEEK WORKSHEET

Name_____

DAY OF THE WEEK, NAME OF EVENT, AND BIBLE VERSES

DIRECTIONS:

1. Look up one or more of the biblical verses which tell about this event and read it. Circle the biblical verses above that you read.

2. Look through your picture file and find as many pictures as you can that illustrate this event.

3. Use a narrow strip of colored construction paper and felt pens to make a title for your event.

4. Use small rolls of masking tape to mount the title and the pictures onto the display board.

5. Make a list of objects, or things that we could use with the display to help us remember what happened.

6. Try to find some of these objects around the house and bring them for the display on Palm Sunday.

7. Think of a model of a 3D scene you could make to illustrate the event. Make one at home by yourself or with a friend.

8. Tell about the event in your own words. You may write a short paragraph that tells about the event and can be fastened to your display, or you may record it on the cassette recorder so that people can listen as they look at your display.

BIBLE VERSES

1. ENTRY INTO JERUSALEM: Matt. 21:1-11; Mark 11:1-11; Luke 19:28-40; John 12:12-19

2. JESUS AT THE TEMPLE: Matt. 21:12-17; Mark 11:15-19 Luke 19:45-48; John 2:13-22

3. JESUS ANOINTED AT BETHANY: Matt. 26:6-13; Mark 14:3-9; John 12:1-8

4. THE LORD'S SUPPER: Matt. 26:26-30; Mark 14:22-26; Luke 22:14-20; 1 Corr. 11:23-25

5. JESUS WASHES DISCIPLES FEET: John 13:1-17

6. JESUS PRAYS IN GETHSEMANE: Matt. 26:36-46; Mark 14:32-42; Luke 22:39-46

7. JESUS' ARREST: Matt. 26:47-56; Mark 14:43-50; John 18:3-11

8. JESUS BEFORE THE COUNCIL: Matt. 26:57-68; Mark 14:53-65; Luke 22:54-55,63-71; John 18:13-14

9. PETER DENIES JESUS: Matt. 26:57-68; Mark 14:53-65; Luke 22:56-62; John 18:15-18,25-27

10. JESUS BEFORE PILATE: Matt. 27:1-2, 11-14; Luke 23:1-5; John 18:28-38;Mark 15:1-5

11. SOLDIERS MAKE FUN OF JESUS:Matt. 27:27-31; Mark 15:16-20; John 19:2-3

12. JESUS IS CRUCIFIED: Matt. 27:32-44; Mark 15:21-32; Luke 23:26-43; John 19:17-27

13. BURIAL OF JESUS: Matt. 27:57-61; Mark 15:42-47; Luke 23:50-56; John 19:38-42

14. THE RESURRECTION: Matt. 28:1-8; Mark 16:1-18; Luke 24:1-12, John 20:1-18

NOTE: Ideas for three dimensional projects might include the following:

PALM SUNDAY: Map which shows the route from Bethany to Jerusalem. Figure riding donkey along a road with palm branches.

CLEANSING THE TEMPLE: Model of the Temple. Doll furniture scene with tables overturned.

TEACHING AT THE TEMPLE: Examples of Biblical coins.

CRUCIFIXION: Model of three crosses on a hill.

BURIAL: Model of rock tomb and stone.

ACROSS THE FIELDS

by Neil C. Fitzgerald

CHARACTERS:

JACOB, husband
MIRIAM, his wife
RACHEL, daughter, age 16
RUBEN, husband's cousin
BENJAMIN, son, age 10

TIME: *The first Easter Sunday morning just after daybreak.*

SETTING: *The home of a poor farmer on the outskirts of Jerusalem. Within the home are a table, two benches, several bowls, and foodstuff. A door to the outside is to the left. The play may be set in a church sanctuary or hall by merely using a door frame to represent the exit*

AT RISE: *MIRIAM is at the table preparing food. RACHEL, standing nearest the doorway, is helping. JACOB stands in the middle of the room stretching his arms above his head. Each is dressed in long robe, headdress, and sandals.*

JACOB: O, what a glorious morning. I am anxious to go out into the fields. *(Looking around)* Where is Benjamin?

MIRIAM: He will be back shortly.

JACOB: Well, where is he? That boy is never around when there is work to be done.

MIRIAM: He went to look for his lost lamb.

RACHEL: Remember, Father, yesterday was the Sabbath, and you wouldn't let him look for it then.

JACOB. He is just wasting precious time. He'll never find the creature. The lamb was either stolen or has been eaten by some animal by now.

MIRIAM: Benjamin said he would be back in time to go into the fields with you.

JACOB *(To RACHEL):* Rachel, look and see if your brother is coming.

RACHEL *(Peering out the doorway):* No sign of Benjamin, but cousin Ruben is headed this way across the fields.

JACOB *(Irritated):* Not again today.

MIRIAM: Jacob, please, be kind to him. Remember how upset he was yesterday.

JACOB: How could I forget? He went on for hours talking about that Jesus and how they crucified him.

RACHEL: But, Father, Jesus was a miracle worker.

JACOB: Did you ever see him work any miracles?

RACHEL: You know I never saw him at all. *(Pause)* But my friend Sarah did.

JACOB: Oh, yes, Sarah. Where was that?

RACHEL: At Bethany.

MIRIAM: You remember, Jacob?

JACOB: All I remember is Sarah rushing in here and telling some wild story.

RACHEL: I think it was a beautiful happening. I wish I had been there. Sarah had gone to Bethany to console Martha and Mary when she had heard about the death of their brother, Lazarus. Sarah said when she arrived in Bethany, there were a great number of people there. Martha, Mary, and the others were gathered around the person they called Jesus. Then Martha, Mary, and their friends followed Jesus to the cave where Lazarus had been buried for four days.

JACOB: Four days?

RACHEL: Yes. And Jesus stood before the cave and shouted, "Lazarus, come out!" And Lazarus came out bound head and foot with linen strips and his face bound with a cloth. Jesus told them to untie him.

JACOB (Cynically): And, of course, Lazarus just walked among them like nothing had happened.

RACHEL: Father, Sarah saw him.

JACOB: That Sarah. Even as a little one she was always full of such unbelievable stories.

MIRIAM: But she's a young lady now like our Rachel.

JACOB: I still don't believe her.

RUBEN (Entering): Forgive the intrusion again of a sorrowful man.

MIRIAM: You know you are always welcome, Ruben.

RUBEN: I just came to rest a spell. I'm on my way to visit his tomb. (Sits)

JACOB: Ruben, you have to regain control of yourself. Life must go on. Besides, how can you mourn so for someone you never even met?

RUBEN: But I saw him.

JACOB: Yes, dead, hanging from a cross.

RUBEN: I saw the soldier drive a lance into his side and blood and water gushed forth. I wish I had come sooner. I learned too late what was happening. They might have let me carry his cross.

JACOB: Ruben, why do you have such devotion to this man?

RUBEN: Because I believe in his teachings. I believe he was more than just a prophet. He performed many miracles.

JACOB: Yet he died like any other man. Can you deny that?

RUBEN: No, I saw him in death. I admit I'm confused. I can't understand why it happened. If only I could have seen him alive and heard his voice like your Benjamin.

JACOB: Benjamin! A fine example he gave to Benjamin. He almost started a riot in the temple.

RUBEN: Now, Jacob, you know some of the prac-

tices that have been going on at the temple are outrageous. I remember your saying that it wasn't right what some were doing, and it certainly could not be pleasing to God.

JACOB: But did Jesus have to overturn the money-changers tables and stalls of the dove sellers?

RUBEN: I'll admit it was dramatic, but something needed to be done.

JACOB: According to Benjamin Jesus said, "My house shall be called a house of prayer but you have turned it into a den of thieves." Why you would think the temple was his personal sanctuary.

RUBEN: Yet you must admit that Benjamin was impressed.

JACOB: Too impressed for my liking.

RUBEN (Rising): I must be on my way. I am anxious to visit his tomb.

MIRIAM: God go with you, Ruben.

BENJAMIN (Bursting into the room): He's alive! He's alive! I saw him!

JACOB: What are you saying, Benjamin?

BENJAMIN: Jesus lives!

RUBEN (Excitedly): You saw him?

BENJAMIN: Yes, just moments ago. I ran all the way home.

RUBEN: Where?

BENJAMIN (Pointing toward the doorway): Out there. On the road to Emmaus.

RUBEN: I must find him. (RUBEN hurries from the room.)

JACOB (Shouting): Ruben, come back here! (Turns to BENJAMIN, grabs him by the arms and shakes him angrily) How could you do that to Ruben? How could you play such a trick on him? You know how distraught he has been these past few days.

BENJAMIN (Pleading): Father, it is no trick. I saw Jesus. I really did.

MIRIAM: Jacob, please.

JACOB: (Letting go of BENJAMIN): You think you saw Jesus. It was probably a man who looked like him.

104

BENJAMIN: No, it was the same Jesus I saw in the temple. I'd know him anywhere. (*JACOB turns away from BENJAMIN.*)

RACHEL: Tell us what happened.

BENJAMIN: I was on my way home from looking for my lamb.

RACHEL: Did you find him?

BENJAMIN: No. Anyway, as I neared the road to Emmaus, I saw two men walking along the road from Jerusalem. Then I saw a third man approach them.

RACHEL: Where was he coming from?

BENJAMIN: I don't really know. All of a sudden he was just there. As I came closer to the road, I recognized him. It was Jesus.

MIRIAM: Did he see you?

BENJAMIN: I don't think so.

RACHEL: So then what happened?

BENJAMIN: The three of them kept walking along the road and I ran home.

RACHEL: That's everything?

BENJAMIN: Yes. (*Pause*) One thing though was strange.

RACHEL: What?

BENJAMIN: The two men with Jesus . . . I am sure I saw them with him that day at the temple.

RACHEL: What's so strange about that?

BENJAMIN: Well, when Jesus met them on the road, they acted like they didn't even know him.

JACOB: Probably because he was some stranger and not Jesus.

BENJAMIN: No, Father, you're wrong. It was Jesus. It was!

RACHEL: Oh, Benjamin, let's try to catch up to Jesus.

JACOB: Children, there's work to be done.

RACHEL: Oh, please, Father, let us go for a little while. Perhaps others have seen Jesus, too.

JACOB: Aren't you even listening to me?

MIRIAM: Let them go, Jacob. At least for a little while.

JACOB (*Throwing up his hands*): My whole family has lost its senses. All right, just for a while.

RACHEL (*Kisses JACOB*): Oh, thank you, Father. (*A lamb's bleating is heard. BENJAMIN runs outside. RACHEL runs to the doorway.*) Benjamin's lamb has come home. (*Note:BENJAMIN could appear at the doorway holding a real lamb if desired.*) Quickly, put your lamb in a safe place. We must hurry if we are to catch up to Jesus . (*Exits*)

JACOB: Such a family. It is a good thing I still have my senses.

MIRIAM: Is that what you call it?

JACOB: What are you saying?

MIRIAM: Nothing.

JACOB: Miriam, I know you. Tell me, what are you really thinking?

MIRIAM: Couldn't we go with the children?

JACOB: In search of Jesus?

MIRIAM: Yes.

JACOB: But what about the land, the house, all that must be done?

MIRIAM: They won't go away.

JACOB: It is foolishness what you propose.

MIRIAM: Perhaps.

JACOB: And if I say no?

MIRIAM: We stay.

JACOB: Yes, we stay and I don't want to hear two words from you the rest of the day. Why do you always do this to me, Miriam?

MIRIAM: Tell me honestly, Jacob, do you believe your son was lying?

JACOB: No, Miriam. When I looked into his eyes, I knew that he believed he acutally saw Jesus.

MIRIAM: And that frightens you.

JACOB (*Softly*): Yes.

MIRIAM: I would like to go, Jacob.

105

JACOB (*Regaining some of his flamboyancy*): Alright, we shall go. And when you and Rachel and Benjamin find out this man on the road to Emmaus is just another passerby, we shall return. And a year from now the world will go on its busy way having forgotten all about this man Jesus who was crucified on a hill no one will even remember.

MIRIAM: We shall see. (*Taking JACOB by the hand*) Come now, my husband, let us follow our children. (*MIRIAM and JACOB exit. Curtain.*)

THE END

PRODUCTION NOTES

Characters: 3 male, 2 female
Playing time: 12 minutes
Costumes: long robes, headdresses, and sandals
Properties: table, two benches, several bowls, food-stuff, and possibly a lamb (see text)
Setting: a room in a farmer's home containing a table, two benches, several bowls, and food-stuff, with a single exit on the left
Lighting: no special effects
Sound: the sound of a lamb bleating

EASTER CELEBRATION

by Elaine M. Ward

Spring is full of God's surprises, but the greatest of all God's surprises is Easter, Christ among us forever. Easter is a time of joyous celebration for all creation, especially for God's children in the church, for Easter is a new beginning. It is the symbol of new relationship with God.

EASTER WORSHIP WITH CHILDREN

Opening Voluntary: Music for Trumpet and/or Organ

Call to Worship:
Worship Leader: Christ is risen!
People: He is risen indeed!

Procession: (Children carrying portable cross and banners made in class on previous Sundays from paper or felt)

Hymn: "Christ the Lord Is Risen Today" (Charles Wesley, Easter Hymn Tune)

Prayer: Worship Leader

Words of Assurance: John 14:2-3

The Lord's Prayer

Offertory: Worship Leader: We offer our gifts of money to be raised as living expressions of our love.

Old Testament Reading: Child reads Job 19:25-27

Hymn: "How Strong and Sure My Father's Care" (Thomas Tallis Tune)

New Testament Reading: John 21:15-17 read as a responsive reading between a Child Leader and the Congregation.

Story Sermon: "The Butterfly"[1]

The small, furry, green caterpillar ate its way up the stalk of grass. Slowly, silently it munched its way. The man on the hill watched the caterpillar. For the first time that day he was alone.

The man sat silently thinking and watching the caterpillar. What was the man thinking as he watched the caterpillar, this strong, silent man? Who was he? From where had he come? Like the caterpillar, where was he going? What was he meant to do? When would he do it? These were the man's thoughts as he sat watching the caterpillar eat, doing what the caterpillar was meant to do.

Some people live quietly, seeking God's will. This man, however, was impatient. He had lived all his life asking God what he must do.

As he watched the caterpillar eat, he remembered that soon it would spin its cocoon and die. This was why it was eating the green leaves.

Suddenly the man knew. He knew what he had to do. Slowly, he arose and left the hill.

107

The city was crowded with people because it was a great holiday. There was much to see and do. The people went to the temple and to the marketplace. Some of the people even went to the hill where the criminals were hung on heavy crosses. This year the people who visited the hill were especially curious, for one of the criminals to be hung was the loving, rebel preacher, a carpenter from Nazareth.

The people shouted when they saw him dragging his cross behind him. "Save yourself, preacher! Remember, you are God's son!" they mocked.

The man did not reply. He had come to die. Soon it would be over.

He remembered the last time he had been on that hill, watching the small caterpillar doing what it must do. It was that day he had decided he, too, must do what he needed to do, no matter what the cost. Today there was no caterpillar to watch. Today he was dragging a cross, for soon he must die.

The man, however, was not afraid. He was not bitter or discouraged, for he knew that God was with him. That day the man died on the hill called Calvary.

Later that night they took his body from the cross and wrapped it in soft white sheets like a cocoon and put it in a tomb.

A few days later, when friends of the man went to the tomb, the white sheets lay on the ground, for the man's body was no longer there. The women wondered and began to cry.

"Why are you crying?" asked a voice behind them.

The women turned, for they thought they recognized the voice. They thought they recognized the man, but he was different, and on his shoulder rested a small, yellow butterfly.

(Prop: a butterfly) Today, Easter, is a joyful, glorious day for worship. The butterfly, shedding its cocoon to fly, has become a symbol of the new life we experience in Christ.

(If the butterfly you have is alive, at the end of the story, release it to fly!)

Benediction: Worship Leader: God, who created the galaxies and all of life, tells us on this Easter day that life goes on. In that hope and with God's love, go out into the world, knowing God is with you. Amen.

1 "The Butterfly", Elaine M. Ward, **Story-telling—With Stories to Tell**. Discipleship Resources Nashville, 1981.

LENTEN AIRWAYS TOURS

by Jane Priewe

Take your youth for a trip on the Lenten Airways. Place chairs in rows, as though it were the inside of an airplane. Have someone act as pilot, and choose a steward and stewardess to help give the tour information. The steward and stewardess can add authenticity by pointing across passengers through imaginary windows.

This would even be a fun project to share with younger children during the Lenten season. Passengers could be ushered on board and greeted by steward and stewardess before the tour begins. At the end of the tour, passengers can deplane in the same manner. This will avoid an unruly departure. If everyone wants to have a part in this presentation, divide your group into smaller groups of three, and let them share the Lenten Airways with small groups in your church school.

Captain:
Lenten Airways welcomes you.
We're glad to have you aboard.
This is your captain speaking.
Our chief pilot is the Lord.
(Girl's name) is your stewardess
She'll help give information.
And so will (boy's name), your steward,
Throughout the flight's duration.
Beneath us is Jerusalem,
A city with a rich past.
I'll circle lower so you'll see
Where palm fronds and cloaks were cast.
When Jesus rode through the town,
People shouted, cheered, and sang.
For this man they called their King,
With excitement, their voices rang.

Steward:
And there you see the temple
Where Jesus fumed and raged,
Upsetting tables, scattering coins,
Freeing anything that was caged.
"My house is called a house of prayer."
He said, "Not a den of thieves!"
Then when he healed the lame and blind,
Priests and scribes were most displeased.

Stewardess:
Two miles from Jerusalem;
That town below, which you see,
Friends of Jesus lived there.
It's the village of Bethany.
It was the home of Lazarus,
Whom Jesus raised from the tomb.
Also Martha, and Mary
Who washed Christ's feet with perfume.

Steward:
Now, back to Jerusalem.
See that small building down there?
It's where Christ held the Last Supper.
Even then he was aware
Of the agony that faced him
When he'd suffer for mankind's sin.
He knew among his disciples
There was a traitor within.

109

Stewardess:
We're passing over Gethsemane
Near the base of the mount down there.
Where Jesus sweated drops of blood
In piercing, painful prayer.
Peter, James, and John slept on,
Too tired to watch or speak.
"The spirit is willing," Christ said,
"But, oh, the flesh is weak."
Then came the Roman soldiers
With Judas leading them.
When he stepped forth to kiss Christ's cheek,
Our Savior, he did condemn.

Steward:
Next on our tour is Golgotha,
Also called Calvary.
Just down there near Damascus Gate
Skull Hill is what you see.
The place where Christ was crucified,
His hands and feet nailed tight,
Where soldiers gambled for his clothes,
And day grew dark as night.
When Jesus died upon the cross,
The heavens flashed and boomed.
The temple veil, it split in half.
Oh, what a day of doom!

Captain:
Now, to your right, see all that green
Not far from Calvary?
In that garden in a tomb
They buried the man from Galilee.
The tomb was sealed, and men stood guard,
For some had heard Christ say,
"After three days, I'll rise again."
They thought he might get away.
No seals or guard could hold *him* in.
No tomb could be *his* prison.
On Sunday morning an angel said,
"He's not here. He is risen!"

Stewardess:
He had suffered for our sins.
His dear life he had given.
But he lives on in all our hearts,
And waits for us in heaven.
As we make our landing
Remember Christ's last days.
We have enjoyed your company,
Thanks for flying Lenten Airways.

LITANY PRAYER OF PRAISE

by Jane Landreth

This prayer of praise will help the boys and girls express worshipful thoughts and thanks to God for giving His son, Jesus.

A litany is a prayer arranged so that there are alternate praise or request lines to God and a response line. The pattern is followed throughout the litany.

In order for the pupils to write such a litany, they must first feel gratitude to God. Discuss with the boys and girls the resurrection of Jesus. Guide the conversation to include the idea that Jesus died for everyone, that Jesus was the best love-gift that God gave.

Ask: For what do you thank God for from the resurrection story? For what do you thank God about Jesus? For what do you thank God about celebrating Easter? Record the answers on a poster board. Between each answer leave enough space to print, "We thank you, O God," or "The Lord is Risen!"

Read the litany together. Divide the pupils to allow one group to read the praise lines (answers) and the remaining pupils to read the response lines.

Plan to snare the litany with another church school class.

An example of a litany might be:
(Praise) For Jesus who gave his life on the cross,
(Response) We thank you, O God.

OR

(Praise) We thank you for Jesus who died on the cross.
(Response) The Lord is Risen!

DOUGH BABIES

by Linda S. Davidson

Serving special food at Easter is a tradition in many families. Add to your church school celebrations a yummy Easter bread that is fun to make and good to eat! Take a trip to the church kitchen. (The teacher may want to prepare the dough ahead of time.)

There are many traditional Easter breads like paska from the Ukraine, hot cross buns from England, the festival loaf from Greece, and babka from Poland. Have your class do some research on these if there is time. Discuss family traditions which they engage in at Easter. What special food does someone's mother always make at Easter? What favorite dishes do they request each year?

Talk about the symbolism of the egg. What does it represent? Why are eggs used so much at Easter? This recipe from the Netherlands has each dough baby hugging an egg. The dough is simple to make and requires no special ingredients. The results are appealing to look at and eat, and in a tangible way help spread Easter joy.

DUTCH EASTER BABIES

1¾ cups plus 1 tbs. milk
¼ cup butter or margarine
2½ teaspoons sugar
2 teaspoons salt
1 package active dry yeast
¼ cup warm water (105-
   115 degrees)
5 to 6 cups flour
9 small eggs
   seedless raisins or
   currants

Scald 1¾ cups milk. Stir in butter, sugar, and salt. Cool to lukewarm. Sprinkle yeast on to warm water in a large warm bowl. Stir until dissolved. Add lukewarm milk mixture and 3 cups flour, beating until smooth. Stir in enough additional flour to make a stiff dough. Turn out onto lightly floured board, knead until smooth and elastic, about 8-10 minutes. Place in greased bowl, turning to grease top. Cover, let rise in a warm place, free from draft, until doubled in bulk, about 1 hour. Punch down dough, turn out onto lightly floured board. Divide dough in 8 pieces. Keep pieces of dough covered until ready for shaping.

Shape one piece into a 5-inch oblong roll. Place a raw small egg on the dough, a little above center. Pretend the egg is the center of a clock. Cut slits at 2, 4, 6, 8, 10 o'clock. Pulling dough, shape arms and legs. Put arms over and across the egg. Shape a round, flat head. Use raisins and currants for eyes, nose, mouth. Repeat with remaining pieces of dough. Place on greased baking sheets.

Combine the remaining egg and 1 tablespoon milk, brush over dough babies. Bake in 400-degree preheated oven 20 minutes or until golden brown and done. Remove from baking sheets and cool on wire racks.

To color eggs, do so after baking. Remove any oily film from the eggs with a cotton swab and vinegar. Brush liquid food color on eggs. Makes 8 dough babies.

STAND-UP BUNNY

by Linda S. Davidson

You will need: pattern for bunny, construction paper, crayons, scissors.

Rabbits have long been a symbol of Easter. Many people believe that the hare or rabbit of Easter is a symbol of new life, as it probably was in religions far older than Christianity.

To make our stand-up bunny, have the children trace the pattern on a folded piece of construction paper. Dotted lines indicate where to fold. Cut out the bunny and fold, as shown in our illustration. Details of the face, basket, and paws may be drawn on with crayon or felt pens, or cut out from construction paper and then glued onto the bunny.

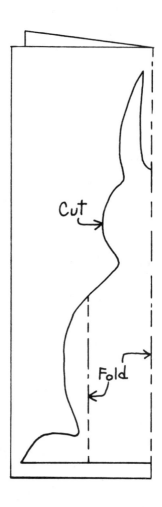

CROSS PROJECTS
by Linda S. Davidson

There are many projects that can be developed around the cross design. Here are a few:

1. Bookmarks: From construction paper, cut a cross about 3 inches by 4 inches, with the crossbars 1 inch wide. Glue rick-rack around the edge. Sequins, glitter, or narrow ribbon may be glued in the center or around the edges.

2. Shell cross: From cardboard, about 5 inches by 7 inches, cut a cross with the crossbars 1½ inches wide. Cover about half of the cross liberally with glue and immediately arrange shell macaroni close together on the glued area. Continue doing the same with the rest of the cross. Leave about 1 inch wide area at the base of the cross.

When the glue is dry, spray paint the cross (gold is very pretty). Tape a string hanger at the back and staple a plastic flower to the unglued area at the base of the cross.

3. Window plaque: In the center of a 7 inch or 8 inch paper plate, draw a cross about 2 inches by 3 inches. Carefully cut out this cross. With glue, draw lines on the plate radiating from the cross opening. Sprinkle with glitter. Edge the plate with rick-rack or other pretty braid. Print or glue a typewritten Bible verse below the cross.

ITALIAN EASTER BREAD

by Linda S. Davidson

Try making a bread ring with your church school class during Lent. If you do not have enough class time, make one at home and bring it to class to share with your young people. Have the class do some research on the Easter customs of several different countries. If you have some helpful mothers, ask them to each make a different Easter bread, and then the class could try celebrating a few Easter customs together.

You will need:

2½ C. all-purpose flour
¼ C. granulated sugar
1 t. salt
1 pkg. active dry yeast
2/3 C. milk
2 T. butter
2 eggs, room temp.

½ C. candied mixed chopped
   fruits
¼ C. chopped blanched
   almonds
   melted butter
5 colored raw eggs

1½ C. powdered sugar
½ C. whipping cream or
   half-and-half
1 t. vanilla
¼ t. salt
   colored candy sprinkles

1. Combine 1 cup of the flour, the granulated sugar, 1 teaspoon salt and the yeast in large mixer bowl. Heat milk and 2 tablespoons butter in small saucepan until lukewarm. (Butter does not have to melt.) Beat milk with butter gradually into flour mixture on medium speed, scraping side of bowl occasionally, 2 minutes. Add 2 eggs and ½ cup of the flour; beat on high speed 2 minutes. Stir in enough of the remaining flour to make a soft dough.

2. Knead dough on lightly floured surface, adding only enough flour to keep dough from sticking, until smooth and elastic, 8-10 minutes. Place in greased large bowl; turn greased side up. Cover with plastic wrap; let rise until double, about 1 hour. Punch down dough.

3. Heat oven to 350 degrees. Combine fruits and nuts in small bowl. Knead fruit mixture into dough. Divide dough in half; roll each half into a 24-inch rope. Twist ropes loosely and form into a ring. Transfer to greased baking sheet. Brush ring with melted butter; place colored eggs in spaces in the the twist. Let rise uncovered until double, about 1 hour. Bake until top is golden, 30-35 minutes. Cool on wire rack, at least 15 minutes.

4. Mix powdered sugar, whipping cream, vanilla and ¼ teaspoon salt in small bowl; stir until smooth, adding cream if frosting is stiff. Paint bread with frosting using pastry brush and decorate with candy sprinkles. Cut bread into wedges and serve with butter.

Makes 1 bread ring.

EASTER LILY STENCIL

by Linda S. Davidson

You will need: construction paper, spray paint, X-acto knife, newspapers.

Lilies and other flowers that grow from bulbs, such as tulips or daffodils, are symbols of the resurrection. The bulb stands for the tomb of Jesus, the blossom for his life after death.

There are many ways to use a stencil, but we would suggest making an Easter card with the stencil in our illustration. Using an X-acto knife or a one-edged razor blade, carefully cut out all the dark areas of our stencil. Next take a piece of 9 x 12" construction paper and fold it in quarters. Put down newspaper for protection. Put the folded card down, then put the stencil on top of it. Now spray paint it. Wait a minute and then slowly remove the stencil. See what a lovely card you have! Inside write your Easter message and sign the card.

114

EGG PROJECTS

by Linda S. Davidson

The miracle of new life-this is the meaning of an Easter egg. It goes back far beyond any one religion and belongs to all mankind.

Here are several ideas for decorating eggs for Easter. First consider a few possibilities of types of eggs to use: plastic panty hose eggs, styrofoam eggs and blown-out egg shells. Obviously the egg shells are the most fragile, so use them with older children.

One simple way to decorate an egg is to glue on small scraps of fabric for a patchwork effect. Small children can do this very easily on plastic or styrofoam eggs, which you can purchase at your local craft store.

Another idea is to use embroidery floss or yarn, etc., wind it around a styrofoam egg. Start at one end of the egg, tack the end of the thread with glue and start wrapping it around and around the egg. When you wish to end one color and begin another, poke the end of the thread with a toothpick under the wound section. We would suggest when you reach the middle, begin again at the other end and meet in the middle. Use glue for problem spots.

Ribbon and trims can be used very effectively to produce lovely eggs. Supply a variety of these materials for your class, and let the children create! Embroidered trim glued lengthwise on styrofoam eggs with velvet ribbon covering the seams with a bow at the top, make exquisite decorations.

A more delicate project is creating egg shell planters. These can be used as gifts, decorations, or table favors. Hospital patients would enjoy these on their trays Easter day. With small scissors carefully remove about one-third of a large egg shell from the pointed end of an egg. Dump egg out. Rinse well, and then dye bright colors. Glue on two one-inch curtain rings to the bottom of each egg. Fill shells with soil leaving at least one-half an inch at the top to allow for watering, and plant with flower or plant seeds. If planting small seedlings or cuttings, stick them almost to the bottom of the shell. Make these well in advance so they will be growing nicely at Easter. You can use egg cartons to grow these in and then add the curtain rings last, if desired.

115

CHICKEN OR AN EGG?
by Linda S. Davidson

You will need: yellow construction paper, crayons, pencils, scissors, and brass fasteners.

Here is a clever egg that will hatch a chick! Make patterns for the egg, head, and legs. Have each child trace and cut out two egg shapes, one head and two legs. On one egg shape cut a jagged crack through the middle. Attach the two egg shapes together at the ends with brass fasteners. In a similar fashion, attach the head and legs. When they are all turned in you have an egg and pull them out and there is a chick! Which came first, the chicken or the egg?

CARDS

by Linda S. Davidson

You will need oil or enamel paints, shallow tin plates, stirrers (straws, pencils, etc.), water, construction paper, newspaper, pens.

Marbleizing is based on the concept that oil and water do not mix. The variety of colors achieved makes a most unusual effect.

Pour about a ½-inch of water in a pie tin, or an old tray with edges, or a jelly roll pan. Pour a couple drops of paint on top of the water. Add other colors if desired. Stir very gently. After swirling it around, use immediately or the enamels will dry up.

Have scraps of paper available for children to experiment with first. Carefully set paper on top of the water. If you do not push it under, the inside of the card, which is up, will remain clean. After a couple of seconds, carefully lift it out of the water. Set on newspaper to dry.

You can probably do two or three cards before you need to add more paint. To change the paint color, gently wipe a paper towel over the water's surface, lifting off the paint film. When completely dry, fold the card and write an Easter greeting inside.

For variation, try a rubber cement resist. To put a word or symbol (cross, egg, lily, etc. for Easter) on the front of the card, paint on that word or design with rubber cement before you marbleize. Let cement dry. Then marbleize as explained above. When completely dry, pull off the cement. When it is all off, the word or symbol will stand out clearly against the marbleized background.

Older children can emphasize lines and patterns in the finished card with felt-tipped pens.

116

IN-JESUS'-STEPS MAP

by Jane Landreth

For this project the boys and girls in your church school will draw an outline map of Jerusalem in the time of Christ. They will enter on it the names of the places associated with the Crucifixion Week. These will include the Garden of Gethsemane, Pilate's Palace, Temple, Golgatha, Upper Room, Mount of Olives, and others.

The boys and girls will draw on these sites a picture or pictures representing the events that took place during the Crucifixion Week. In addition they will trace the route taken by Jesus as he moved from place to place during that time. The route can be shown by drawing in small footsteps.

For research on this project, pictures, the Bible, Bible storybooks, and other reference books may be used.

Some of the boys and girls may want to prepare a companion map of present day Jerusalem to go along with the biblical one. Such maps may be found in dictionaries, news magazines, encyclopedias, and travel magazines.

The making of the "In-Jesus'-Steps Map" will make the events of the Crucifixion Week come alive for the boys and girls.

BUNNY BASKET

by Linda S. Davidson

You will need: Construction paper, bunny basket pattern, pencils, crayons, scissors, glue, cotton balls, Easter "grass", candy, eggs, or whatever you are going to put in the baskets.

If possible, mimeograph the bunny basket pattern on construction paper before class. If that is not possible, have the children trace the pattern on a piece of construction paper. Let them color in as much detail as they wish with crayons. Cut out the basket and handle. Glue on a cotton ball for the tail at the center of the lower portion of the basket. Cut the four slits for the tabs and fold on the two fold lines. Bend into basket shape and add the handle. Staple together. Add grass and goodies and you have a Bunny Basket!

PICTORIAL CALENDAR

by Jane Landreth

This project will be an eight day calendar, picturing the events that occurred in Jesus' life starting with the triumphal entry into Jerusalem through the resurrection. The day to day events covered in the eight day period are:

Sunday – Triumphal entry into Jerusalem
  (Matthew 21:1-9).
Monday – Cleansing of the Temple
  (Mark 11:15-18)
Tuesday – Teaching in the Temple
  (Mark 11:27-33)
Wednesday – Day of rest in Bethany
  (no activity reported)
Thursday – The Lord's Supper, prayer in the
  garden, the arrest
  (Matthew 26:17-56)
Friday – Crucifixion and burial
  (Matthew 27:1-61)
Saturday – Sealed tomb
  (Matthew 27:62-66)
Sunday – Resurrection
  (Luke 24)

For the calenders, the boys and girls will need paper or posterboard wide enough for eight columns. In each column they will enter a brief description of Jesus' activities for that day or a simple drawing illustrating it. Across the top of the calendar they will write "April A.D. 30" (or whatever date it happens that Easter falls on).

Pupils may get ideas for the drawings from pictures or books. Some pupils may prefer to use symbolic drawings rather than scenes: a palm branch for the triumphal entry, hands breaking bread for the Lord's Supper, three crosses on a hill, an empty tomb, and so on. Such objects will convey events adequately.

Other boys and girls might prefer to write in the columns only descriptions of the happenings and draw descriptive pictures around the sides of the calendars. The children can decide for themselves what they want to use.

Plan the work so that all the boys and girls will have time to enter on their calendars all the activities that took place on the eight days.

EASTER CARDS

by Linda S. Davidson

You will need: scraps of construction paper, 9 x 12" construction paper, glue, pencils, crayons.

First fold the 9 x 12" in half. With a pencil lightly sketch in the outline of a cross. Using several colors of DARK construction paper, tear them into little small pieces. Glue them onto the cross in a mosaic fashion.

Then with LIGHT colors of scraps, fill in the entire background that is left. Younger children may need a lot of time for this. Older children can create their own mosaics using other symbols or designs appropriate to Easter.

To finish the card, write an Easter greeting on the inside and sign the card.

ABOUT THE AUTHORS

BACON, JANICE
Janice Bacon lives in Hingham, MA, where she is Church School Coordinator for the Hingham Congregational Church. She also teaches tennis, is a hospice volunteer, and a freelance writer.

BAGNULL, MARLENE
Marlene Bagnull is a homemaker and freelance writer. She and her husband have three children. She has been active in church school work for many years and lives in Drexel Hill, Pennsylvania.

BLODGET, BENJAMIN B.
Benjamin B. Blodget is a freelance writer who has served as the Director of Christian Education in various churches. He now serves on the Division of Christian Education and the Outdoor Ministries Committee of the Maine Conference, UCC. He lives in Bucksport, Maine.

BRITTON, COLLEEN
Colleen Britton is the Assistant to the Pastor and Coordinator of Christian Education at the Church of the New Covenant in Vacaville, CA. She is an artist, teacher, photographer, and freelance writer, her latest book being, *Celebrate Communion,* a resource and study guide for church school classes on the subject of communion.

DAVIDSON, LINDA
Linda Davidson is on the staff of Educational Ministries, Inc.

DAVIDSON, ROBERT G.
Robert G. Davidson is an ordained minister in the United Church of Christ. He is editor and publisher of the **CHURCH EDUCATOR**, a national monthly publication for Christian educators. It is published by Educational Ministries, Inc., of which he is the founder and president.

EDWARDS, STEVEN L.
Steven L. Edwards is the Minister of Education at the Prairie Baptist Church, Prairie Village, KS.

FITZGERALD, NEIL C.
Neil C. Fitzgerald has been an English teacher for the New Bedford MA, school system for over twenty years. His poetry and articles have appeared in over 80 publications.

FRENZ, JUDITH
Judith Frenz is the Parish Resource Person at the Bethany Lutheran Church, Tucson, AZ.

GLENNIE, JANNEL
Jannel Glennie is Director of Christian Education for the United Presbyterian Church of Okemos and the First Presbyterian Church of Mason, Michigan.

HOOLEY, ELAINE OWEN
Elaine Owne Hooley is a freelance writer from Richmond, Virginia.

IRWIN, PAUL B.

Dr. Paul B. Irwin is Professor Emeritus of Christian Education, School of Theology, Claremont, California.

KILLIAN, IDA F.

Ida F. Killian has written extensively for several church periodicals and has served in many positions in her local church's educational program in Cap May, New Jersey.

LANDRETH, JANE

Jane Landreth is a freelance writer who contributes regularly to several religious education publications. She lives in Clever, Missouri.

PRIEWE, JANE

Jane Priewe is a freelance writer whose articles have appeared in many national educational publications. She lives in Alhambra, CA.

RASMUSSEN, JEAN

Jean Rasmussen is a freelance writer and is active in the Christian education department of the Southwood Baptist Church. She lives in Wenonah, New Jersey.

ROSQUIST, VIVIAN J.

Vivian J. Rosquist is a freelance writer from Missoula, Montana.

TAYLOR, WESLEY D.

Dr. Wesley D. Taylor is a minister at the First United Methodist Church, Oregon City, Oregon.

THOMAS, RUDY H.

Rudy H. Thomas is the minister of the Dover Congregational Church, UCC, Westlake, Ohio.

WARD, Elaine M.

Elaine M. Ward is a Christian educator who believes in the power of the story to feed the spirt, challenge the will, comfort and heal the wounds. As Director of University Park United Methodist Church Weekday School, she writes and shares stories with children, youth, and adults. She is also a contributing editor of *Church Educator* and *Church Teacher.* She lives in Dallas, Texas.

WATKINS, MARK E.

Mark E. Watkins is the minister of the Community Christian Church, Riverdale, Georgia. He also serves as the Youth Advisor in Georgia for the Christian Church (Disciples of Christ) and as a chaplain at the Hartsfield International Airport. Mark is also an actor.